The Pocket Chart Book

by Valerie SchifferDanoff

S C H O L A S T I C
PROFESSIONAL BOOKS

New York • Toronto • London • Auckland • Sydney

Dedication

This book is dedicated to my sons, because I love you so much and wish you continued educational success. I hope this book will help teachers teach other sons and daughters.

Acknowledgments

I wish to acknowledge the following people: Terry Cooper, Editor in Chief of Scholastic Professional Books, for her foresight; Virginia Dooley, Scholastic editor, for her insight; Jaime Lucero, Scholastic designer, for his ability to sight and highlight.

Thank you to the Westchester Teacher Center (Hartsdale, NY), a space for teachers to share with teachers.

Copyright Acknowledgments

"The Butterfly" by Clinton Scollard appeared originally in CHILD LIFE MAGAZINE. Copyright © 1924, 1952 by Rand McNally & Company. Reprinted by permission of Rand McNally & Company.

"Hamsters" by Marci Ridlon. Copyright Marci Ridlon. Reprinted by permission of the author.

"Five little goblins on a Halloween night..." from HAND RHYMES collected by Marc Brown. Copyright © 1985 by Marc Brown. Reprinted by permission of Penguin Books USA.

"There Once Was a Puffin" by Florence Page Jacque from CHILD LIFE MAGAZINE. Copyright © 1930, 1958 by Rand McNally & Company. Reprinted by permission of The Nature Conservancy.

"Five Little Monsters" from BLACKBERRY INK by Eve Merriam. Copyright © 1985 by Eve Merriam. (A Morrow Junior Book.) Reprinted by permission of Marian Reiner.

Cover design by Vincent Ceci and Jaime Lucero
Designed by Jaime Lucero and Robert Dominguez for Grafica, Inc.
Illustrations by Maxie Chambliss and Robert Dominguez

ISBN 0-590-59927-5
Copyright © 1996 by Valerie SchifferDanoff. All rights reserved.
Printed in the U.S.A.

12 11 10 9 8 7 6 5 4 3 2 1   6 7 8/9

Table of Contents

Table of Contents

Preface

The idea for *The Pocket Chart Book* grew out of my first book, *The Scholastic Integrated Language Arts Resource Book*. Throughout that book there are examples of how to use pocket charts in various ways and places in the classroom. This book focuses on pocket charts and their uses. As a child watcher in my own classroom, I've observed how much children love to be active participants in their own learning. Children and many adults as well, are multisensory learners. Children love to touch and manipulate the things from which they are learning. Empowering children by brainstorming ideas allows their minds to be active as well. Your classroom can become a forum for the thoughts of many as each child contributes his or her own experiences. Children can take ownership of their learning too, as they touch the very piece of paper which becomes part of the group learning process. Children are delighted and excited about a presentation that can change and become the many possibilities that I describe in the pages that follow. Discover the fun of pocket charts as you create some of your own.

Introduction

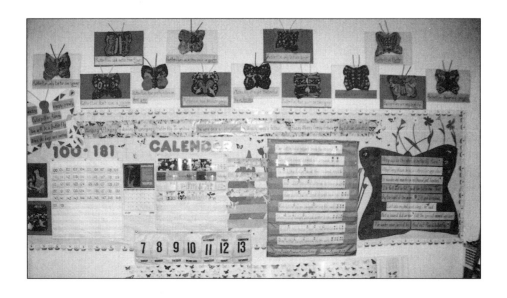

Why Use Pocket Charts?

Pocket charts and sentence strips are two of the most versatile teaching tools for a print-rich classroom. Pocket charts and sentence strips go together like a stamp on a letter. While you can have one without the other, I highly recommend using them together. The pocket chart provides a natural boundary for displays in your classroom, even when a large bulletin board is filled, as the one shown above.

Children love pocket charts, and pocket charts love children. Why? Because pocket charts are virtually indestructible and can be hung at a height just right for young children to reach. Children love to touch and manipulate the words and shapes in pocket charts. You and your children will love the colorful, quick and easy displays pocket charts can create in your classroom.

Pocket charts work for all curriculum areas. They're a natural for all kinds of language arts activities. Written language looks great displayed on different color sentence strips set against different background colors provided by the pocket charts. For teaching dramatic play, you can write dialogue and narration on sentence strips in two different colors. The colors can also teach about quotation marks. For poetry, you can write verses in alternating colors or write rhyming words in matching colors. For art activities, you can write directions on sentence strips and store pieces and templates in the charts. For math, pocket charts provide a manipulative hands-on format. A pocket chart for special days can become a classroom tradition as children anticipate seeing it again and again or having it filled with something new.

Oh Where, Oh Where Can My Pocket Chart Go?

Pocket charts can be used anywhere in the classroom where you would like a poem, a center, an independent learning activity or a follow-up to a large group shared reading or small group guided reading experience.

How Can I Hang My Pocket Chart?

Pocket charts can be displayed on a bulletin board, secured by long heavy-duty push pins, or they can be hung from an easel with easel clips. Heavy-duty self-adhesive Velcro can also be used to hang pocket charts on walls or from shelves. Pocket chart stands are also available at teaching supply stores.

You may find that pocket charts tend to roll inward when suspended. Placing a thin dowel cut to the width of the pocket chart in the last pocket, behind the sentence strip can alleviate this problem. Dowels can be purchased at hardware or home stores or craft shops and cut to size.

What Sizes of Pocket Charts and Sentence Strips Are Available?

Pocket charts are available in a variety of sizes and colors as are sentence strips. If you cannot afford more than one pocket chart, one is a good place to begin. The most versatile size is 42″ x 58″. However, purchasing more than one will prove to be one of the best investments you'll make for your language immersion program.

Other sizes available are 24″ x 24″ and 34″ x 42″. (The most common size for pocket charts is 34″ x 42″.) The best source for purchasing pocket charts and sentence strips is the Teaching Resource Center Catalog. This catalog can be obtained by calling 1-800-833-3389. Red, pink, lavender, blue, yellow, green and white pocket charts in various sizes are available in the catalog.

The best sentence strips for use in a pocket chart are tag quality, precut to 3″ x 24″. They come in white, manila and packs of assorted pastel colors. While rolls of paper are available and cheaper, the money you save is not worth the aggravation of straightening them out.

Pocket Chart Supplies and Sources

American Academic Supplies (1-800-325-9118) offers the following:

- permanent markers, push pins, easel clips
  (Papermate bullet point markers work very well and are available at large discount office supply stores such as Staples and Office Max. You can also find them in some of the catalogs listed below.)

- pocket charts (limited sizes, blue only), sentence strips, glitter writers, stickers, borders, tagboard, pregummed shapes, craft glue, Tru-Ray construction paper, multicultural construction paper, small manipulatives

- Some supplies are also available from the following catalogs:
  J.L. Hammet Co. 1-800-333-4600
  The Reprint Corp. 1-800-248-9171 (good pastel sentence strips)
  Kaplan 1-800-334-2014
  Lakeshore 1-800-421-5354

How to Set Up a Pocket Chart

- Write sentences and words to model handwriting. Do not try to squeeze more words on a sentence strip than will fit. Allow for spaces between words so that words are clearly definable.

- If you run out of room in the pocket chart, you can tack, tape or attach (with paper clips or easel clips) more words above or below the pockets.

- Use permanent markers and tag quality sentence strips.

- Use markers in different colors on white sentence strips to show changes in verse or to highlight steps in a series of directions. Avoid using black marker on white sentence strips as this can sometimes create an optical illusion for young children.

- Use sentence strips in different colors to highlight and teach dialogue in a finger play or poem.

- Use sentence strips in alternating colors to show rhyming couplets in a poem. Using sentence strips in different colors also creates a livelier display.

- Trim off the excess ends of sentence strips and save them to write on when brainstorming or setting up a pocket chart with single words.

- Label templates you use so children can match the words on the labels to words in directions. This will help them to learn words and spelling as they use the templates.

- Use stickers and drawings as rebuses on sentence strips for decorations and to add to understanding.

- For poems, number the sentence strips on the reverse side so you can quickly determine the order of the lines of poetry when you set up the chart.

Basic Teaching Techniques When Teaching from a Pocket Chart

The chapters that follow present pocket charts for language arts, special days and seasons, making things, math, poetry and an integrated unit. You can apply these basic techniques accordingly.

• Model how to use the components in the pocket chart.

• Teach children how to place words, sentence strips and templates in the pocket chart and how to carefully remove them.

• When brainstorming to create a pocket chart, encourage everyone to participate.

• Write words on sentences strips and cut them apart if necessary. As an alternative, have children cut the words apart and then place them in the pocket chart.

• When reading from a pocket chart, read chorally with children. Point to every word as you read.

• When teaching a short poem, chanting or repeating the verses or rhymes is enjoyable. Then encourage children to chant or repeat the poem to the natural rhythm that occurs. Children like to chant sets of rhyming words too.

• When teaching a poem or reading, write two sets of the words. Cut one set apart for children to match words or sequence. As an independent or group activity allow the children to repeat building the story.

• Use pictures in addition to or instead of words. This allows children to match words to pictures and pictures to words. Patterns for templates are provided for this type of activity and stickers are also suggested.

• For math activities use cutouts or stickers as manipulatives. They can be matched to the words.

Additional techniques, hints and reminders are presented with each pocket chart developed in the chapters that follow. By pairing these basic teaching techniques with the examples in each chapter, you can extend and develop more ideas for teaching with pocket charts.

More Resources for Poems

You might want to explore the following resources, too.

The Scholastic Integrated Language Arts Resource Book by Valerie SchifferDanoff (Scholastic Professional Books, 1995)

Building Literacy with Interactive Charts by Kristin Schlosser and Vicki L. Phillips (Scholastic Professional Books, 1992)

Animal Poems from A to Z by Meish Goldish (Scholastic Professional Books, 1995)

Thematic Poems, Songs, and Fingerplays by Meish Goldish (Scholastic Professional Books, 1994)

Read A-Loud Rhymes for the Very Young selected by Jack Prelutsky (Alfred A. Knopf, 1986)

Poems Just For Us! by Bobbi Katz (Scholastic Professional Books, 1995)

Poems You Can Count On by Sandra Liatsos (Scholastic Professional Books, 1995)

Sing A Song of Popcorn selected by Beatrice Schenk De Regniers (Scholastic, 1988)

Blackberry Ink by Eve Merriam (William Morrow, 1985)

Hailstones and Halibut Bones by Mary O'Neill (Bantam, 1961)

Hand Rhymes collected by Marc Brown (Penguin, 1985)

Play Rhymes collected by Marc Brown (Penguin, 1987)

The Random House Book of Poetry selected by Jack Prelutsky (Random House, 1983)

Poetry Place Anthology (Scholastic, 1983)

CHAPTER ONE

Pocket Charts for Language Arts

Language immersion is easy when your classroom is filled with pocket charts, especially ones that build language arts experiences while children have fun!

Build a Snowman

Purpose: To build a snowman by matching words in pocket chart sentences to words displayed with snowman decorations.

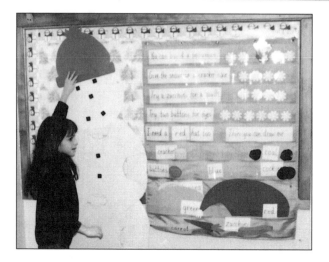

 **Materials**

- 34″ x 42″ pocket chart
- 2-3 sheets of 22″ x 28″ white tagboard (at least 4-ply)
- Sheets of tagboard in blue, red, orange, green, pink, brown, yellow and black (at least 4-ply)
- Tacky glue or other strong paper craft glue
- 10 tag quality sentence strips
- Self-adhesive Velcro (available in rolls at fabric stores)
- Markers and/or crayons
- 8 1/2″ x 11″ sheets of drawing paper, manuscript paper or story paper (no lines on the top half)
- Scissors
- Snowman decoration patterns (See pages 14-15.)

Pocket Chart Words

You can build a snowman.
Give the snowman a _____ nose.
Try a _____ for a mouth.
Try two _____ for eyes.
I need a _____ hat too.
Then you can draw me.

Words for Snowman Decorations

Write two sets:
carrot, zucchini, banana, cookies, coal, buttons, crackers, red, blue, green

Setup

1. From the white tagboard cut a small, medium and large circle. The size of the circles depends on the space you have available for the display. The circles pictured vary in size from 16″ to 22″ in diameter.

2. Overlap and glue the edges of the three circles to create a snowman.

3. Stick one-inch squares of Velcro where a hat, eyes, nose, mouth and buttons would be placed on the snowman. (Be sure to use one side of the Velcro for the display itself and the other side of the Velcro for the items.)

4. From the various colors of tagboard use the patterns to trace and cut out a carrot, a zucchini, a banana, buttons, cookies, crackers, coals, a red hat, a blue hat and a green hat. Fasten the other side of the Velcro to each of these. (You'll need more of this one side of the Velcro than you used on the snowman. Save the excess for another activity.)

5. Write the pocket chart sentences and words on sentence strips in two different colors. Leave spaces or cut sentence strips so that snowman decoration words can be inserted and changed on a daily or weekly basis.

6. Use one set of words to complete the sentences. Place the sentences in the chart. Put the matching words near the snowman decorations below the sentences. Save the other set of words to change in the sentences to vary the word match activity.

7. Place the snowman nearby and at a level children can reach.

Variations

1. Children can copy the sentences about the snowman for handwriting practice.

2. Children can create their own snowman, insert the correct words in the pocket chart sentences and then copy the sentences.

Literature Integrations

Sadie and the Snowman by Allen Morgan (Kids Can Press, 1985)

Bob the Snowman by Sylvia Loretan (Penguin, 1988)

The Mystery of the Missing Red Mitten by Steven Kellogg (Dial, 1974)

The Black Snowman by Phil Mendez (Scholastic, 1989)

Poetry Integrations

"Snowfall" by Margaret Hillert from *Poetry Place Anthology* (Scholastic, 1983)

"Five Sparkling Snowmen" by Valerie SchifferDanoff (See page 39.)

"I Built a Little Snowman" author unknown from *The Scholastic Integrated Language Arts Resource Book* (Scholastic, 1995)

Build A Snowman

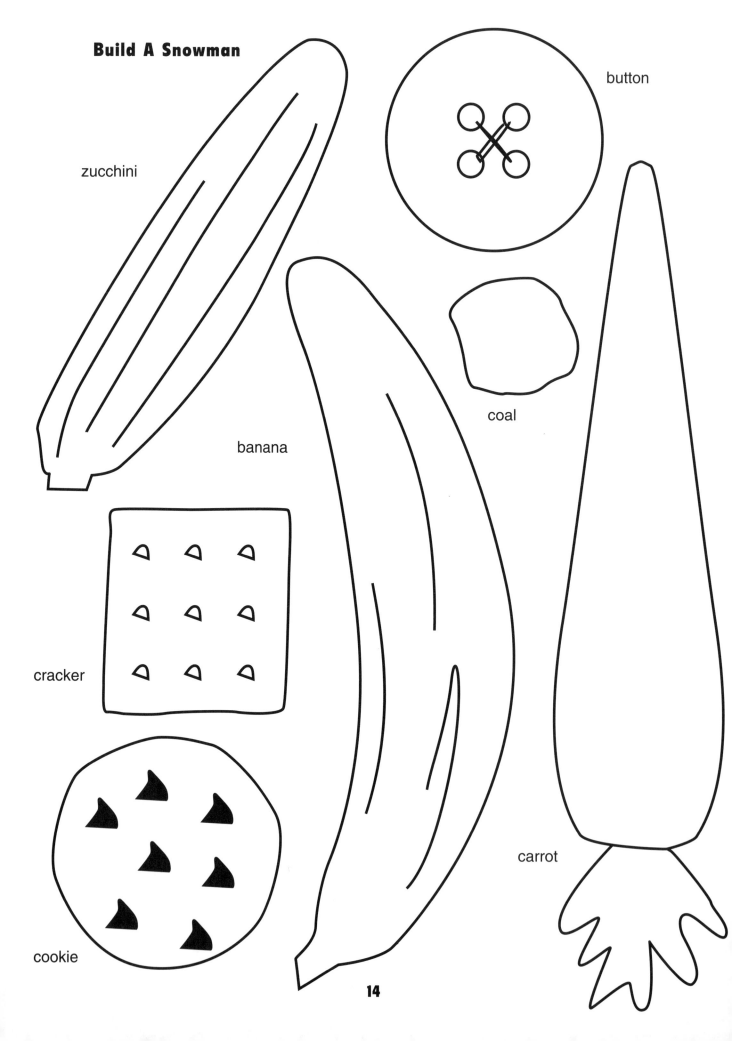

zucchini

button

banana

coal

cracker

carrot

cookie

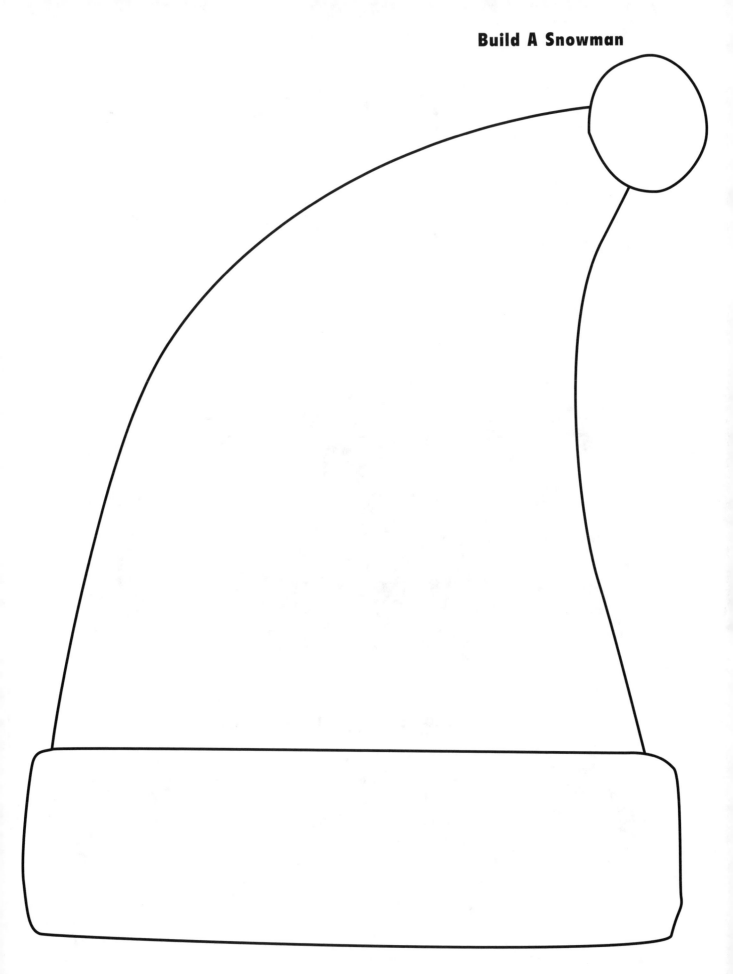

Five Little Penguins

Purpose: To increase reading fluency and develop expressive language and learn about the use of quotation marks for dialogue by reciting a poem for dramatic play.

 **Materials**

- 34″ x 42″ pocket chart
- 10-12 tag quality sentence strips in different colors
- Penguin patterns (See page 18.)
- Scissors
- Tagboard for penguin template
- Permanent markers
- Crayons

Pocket Chart Words

"Five Little Penguins"
by Valerie SchifferDanoff

Five little penguins
Standing in a row
One, two, three, four, five they go!
"I can slide on the ice," said penguin
    number one.
Said penguin number two, "I can hop
    and run!"
"I'm going for a swim," said penguin
    number three.
Said penguin number four, "We catch
    fish at sea."
"I've got an egg to warm," said pen-
    guin number five.
"A new baby chick will soon arrive."
Five little penguins
Huddle together.
They keep warm in any weather.

◆ ■ ◆ Setup ◆ ■ ◆

1. Write the narrated parts of the poem on sentence strips of one color. Then write the penguin dialogue on the other color sentence strips.

2. Trace the penguin patterns on tagboard and then color and cut them out or have children draw the penguins.

3. Place the sentence strips and penguins in the chart to tell the poem. (See the photo on page 16.)

4. After reading the poem chorally with children, have five children each say one of the five speaking penguin parts, while the remaining members of your class narrate the other parts of the poem.

◆ ■ ◆ Literature Integrations ◆ ■ ◆

Antarctica by Helen Cowcher (Farrar, Straus & Giroux, 1990)

A Tale of Antarctica by Ulco Glimmerveen (Ashton Scholastic, 1989)

Tacky the Penguin by Helen Lester (Houghton Mifflin, 1988)

Little Penguin's Tale by Audrey Wood (Harcourt Brace, 1989)

Five Little Penguins

Rewriting Simple Books

Purpose: To increase word knowledge, develop sequencing skills and build understanding of basic concepts by manipulating words, phrases and simple pictures in a pocket chart while retelling a story.

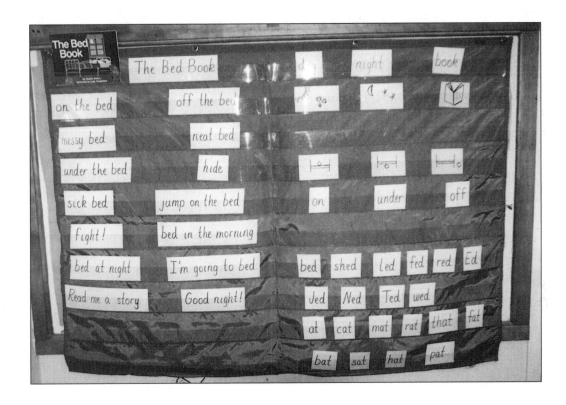

Materials

- 34" x 42" or 58" x 42" pocket chart
- A simple book like *The Bed Book* by Harriet Ziefert (Scholastic, 1981) (See the photograph above.)
- 14 tag quality sentence strips
- Permanent markers
- Scissors

Pocket Chart Words

- words or phrases from each page of the book (See photograph above.)
- words to build language concepts and for visual discrimination
- rhyming words (written from children's responses)

Setup

1. Read the book with children.

2. Reread the book writing the sentences page by page. As you proceed, cut the sentence strips apart and hand the words to children.

3. Once the book is completed, read it again. Have children place words and phrases in the pocket chart as you read. Children can repeat the process on their own for independent follow-up. (See the *Introduction*, Basic Teaching Techniques When Teaching from a Pocket Chart.)

4. For concept building, write one word on small pieces of sentence strips (for example, *day, night, book, on, under, off*) and draw or have children draw a simple picture to match each word. Hand these out to different children. Have children place the words and corresponding pictures in the pocket chart. Children can repeat this activity for independent follow-up.

5. For rhyming words, write two words from the book on sentence strips. Ask children to take turns telling you words that rhyme with these words. Write these words too. Then cut the words apart and hand them out to children. Have children come up to the pocket chart and place the rhyming words together. Children can repeat the activity for independent follow-up.

Literature Integrations

Have you Seen My Cat? by Eric Carle (Picture Book Studio, 1987)

Flying by Donald Crews (William Morrow, 1986)

Who Is Tapping At My Window? by A.G. Deming (Penguin, 1988)

In the Small, Small Pond by Denise Fleming (Henry Holt and Co., 1993)

The Chick and the Duckling by Mirra Ginsburg (Aladdin, 1972)

Rain by Robert Kalan (Greenwillow Books, 1978)

Halloween Cats by Jean Marzollo (Scholastic, 1992)

The Bath Book by Harriet Ziefert (Scholastic, 1981)

Rainbow Heart

Purpose: To learn color words, practice following directions and recognize or develop the concept of size order by cutting and gluing a rainbow heart of different sizes and colors together.

 **Materials**

- 34" x 42" pocket chart
- 3 white or manila tag quality sentence strips, and 1 each in pink, blue, orange, yellow and green
- Heart patterns (See page 23.)
- Manila tagboard for templates
- Scissors
- Glue

- Red, black, purple, green, blue and orange permanent markers
- Sheets of 12" x 18" construction paper in red, orange, yellow, green, blue and violet
- Heart stickers in different colors to decorate sentence strips

Pocket Chart Words

Rainbow Heart

1. Trace and cut a red heart.
2. Trace and cut an orange heart.
3. Trace and cut a yellow heart.
4. Trace and cut a green heart.
5. Trace and cut a blue heart.
6. Trace and cut a purple heart.
7. Glue your hearts together in size order.

 **Setup**

1. Write the directions for making each rainbow heart using markers and sentence strips of the same color. In the case of red, write it with red marker on a pink strip. For purple, write it with purple marker on a white strip. For yellow, use a black marker on a yellow strip. Write non-color directions on manila or white sentence strips.

2. Cut out and trace the paper heart patterns onto tagboard and cut them out. Label templates with the corresponding color word.

3. Arrange the templates and the sentences in the pocket chart as shown in the photograph on page 21.

4. Cut 12″ x 18″ construction paper appropriately for the various sizes of hearts. (The amount of each color will depend on the number of children in your class.) Place the paper near the pocket chart.

5. Have children use the templates and follow the directions in the pocket chart to make a rainbow heart in size order. The completed project is self checking by size and color order.

Literature Integrations

Four Valentines in a Rainstorm by Felecia Bond (Harper & Row, 1983)

A Rainbow of My Very Own by Don Freeman (Penguin, 1966)

Rainbow Crow retold by Nancy Van Laan (Alfred A. Knopf, 1989)

What a Wonderful World by George David Weiss and Bob Thiele (Simon & Schuster, 1995)

Raindrops and Rainbows by Rose Wyler (Simon & Schuster, 1989)

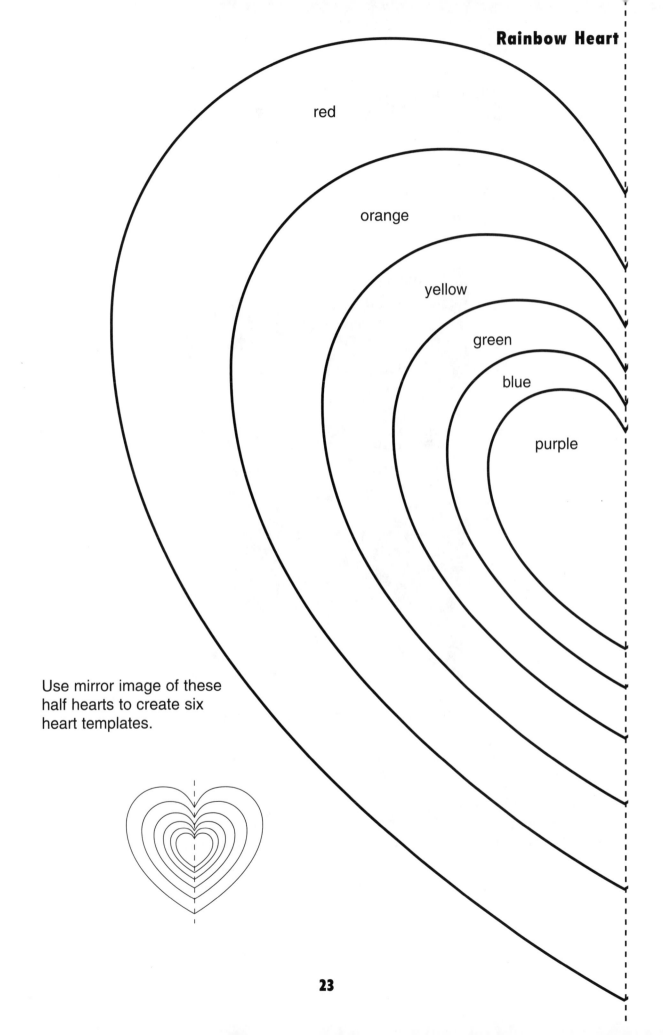

red

orange

yellow

green

blue

purple

Use mirror image of these half hearts to create six heart templates.

There Once Was a Puffin

Purpose: To experience poetry and learn rhyming words by reading and chorally chanting a delightful catchy poem that tells a story.

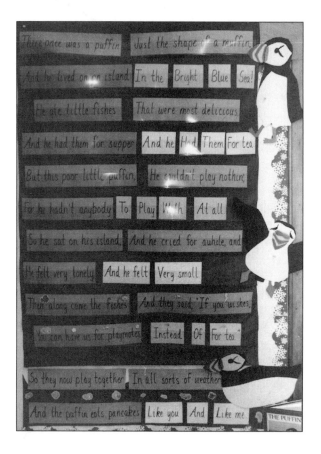

 **Materials**

- 34″ x 42″ pocket chart (plus a little extra space)
- 18 orange, 3 blue and 3 yellow tag quality sentence strips, or sentence strips in three other colors
- Fish stickers
- Optional: pictures of puffins or puffins cut from construction paper

(See templates on pages 63-65.)

Hint: Puffins are not a commonly seen bird unless you live in Maine or further north, so be sure to show pictures of these birds to children. See *Literature Integrations* below for book suggestions and check bird guides.

Pocket Chart Words

"There Once Was a Puffin"
by Florence Page Jacque

There once was a puffin,
  Just the shape of a muffin,
And he lived on an island
  In the bright blue sea!
He ate little fishes
  That were most delicious.
And he had them for supper
  And he had them For tea.
But this poor little puffin,
  He couldn't play nothin,'
For he hadn't anybody
  To play with at all
So he sat on his island,
  And he cried for awhile, and
He felt very lonely,
  And he felt very small.
Then along came the fishes
  And they said, "If you wishes,
You can have us for playmates,
  Instead of for tea."
So they now play together
  In all sorts of weather
And the puffin eats pancakes
  Like you and like me.

 Setup

1. Write the main body of the poem on orange sentence strips.

2. Write the rhyming words alternating on blue and yellow sentence strips. This will highlight the rhyming parts. Cut sentence strips as shown in the photograph to imitate the original, written arrangement of the poem.

3. Apply fish stickers on sentence strips where appropriate.

4. Place the sentence strips in the pocket chart. Tack or staple the extra sentences below the pocket chart.

Variations

1. Children love this poem so they'll be very motivated to copy it for handwriting practice and to illustrate.

2. Create your own class big book using sentence strips glued to white or blue sheets of 12" x 18" construction paper. Have children illustrate each page. You can cut and glue pictures drawn by each child onto the pages.

3. See page 61 and create a "puffinry" around your poem display.

Literature Integrations

Puffin's Homecoming The Story of an Atlantic Puffin by Darcie Bailer (Trudy Management Corporation, 1993)

The Puffins are Back! by Gail Gibbons (HarperCollins, 1991)

The Eye of the Needle retold by Teri Sloat (Penguin, 1990)

Writing a Rainbow

Purpose: To write a poem based on the colors of the rainbow using color words, attributes or senses of colors and items of each color.

Materials

- 7 34" x 42" pocket charts in different colors
- About 70 white tag quality sentence strips
- Red, orange, yellow, green, blue and violet markers
- Scissors
- Colored pencils
- 1-2 sheets of manuscript paper per child

Hint: If possible borrow some pocket charts in different colors from fellow teachers if need be and promise to return the favor as you share the idea too. This activity can be completed using one pocket chart at a time. See *Variations* on page 27.

Pocket Chart Words

- color words
- **words you write when brainstorming with children**

 Setup

1. Hang the seven different colored pocket charts across one long wall.

2. Prewrite each color word on a sentence strip.

3. For each color, brainstorm with children attributes or senses of colors and items that are the color. For example, attributes for red might be: hot, flashy, fast, sweet, bright, warm, sticky, juicy. Red items might be: fire truck, azalea, cherry, strawberry, apple, clay, watermelon, cardinals.

Hint: Try to steer children away from too many items that are artificially colored like T-shirts, markers or crayons. Ask them to think of things in nature that are "naturally colored." You may want to read one selection from *Literature Integrations* below first to get children thinking.

4. As you brainstorm words for each color write the words with the corresponding color marker on sentence strips. You need not limit your class to just the colors of the rainbow.

5. Have children cut words and place them in the chart. If possible use one chart for each color.

6. Discuss and model possible frames for poems in which children write about each of the colors. If you are writing about spring, a possible frame might be:

> **Spring is a rainbow.**
> **Spring is red.**
> **Fast, bright, sweet red.**
> **Hummingbird, azalea, water-melon red.**

Children continue with each color of the rainbow choosing three attribute words and three item words to use in their phrases.

7. Invite children to copy and write words from the pocket chart onto manuscript paper using colored pencils. Their writing will reflect the rainbow.

8. You can display the poems with the rainbow hearts on page 21.

◆ ■ ◆ Variations ◆ ■ ◆

1. Group children cooperatively into seven groups of two to four children. Assign each group a color. Have each group choose words from the chart that describe the assigned color. Then have each group illustrate its color phrases to create a class big book. You can glue the sentence strip words and illustrations to sheets of 12″ x 18″ paper.

2. Have each child choose a color and two words about that color to illustrate. You can glue the sentence strip words onto sheets of 12″ x 18″ paper and then cut and glue children's drawings to create a class big book about colors.

3. Create a rainbow mural bulletin board. Arrange children's sentence strip words and corresponding illustrations in the shape of a large rainbow. Have children draw themselves to be placed under or around the rainbow.

4. Brainstorm words for one color, one day at a time instead of all at once. Each day, have children write about that color.

5. Limit writing and descriptive words to foods. When children complete their writing, have a rainbow food party. (See the photograph on this page.)

◆ ◆ ◆ **Literature** ◆ ◆ ◆
Integrations

Eating the Alphabet by Lois Ehlert (Harcourt Brace Jovanovich, 1989)

Planting a Rainbow by Lois Ehlert (Harcourt Brace Jovanovich, 1988)

Hailstones and Halibut Bones by Mary O'Neill (Doubleday, 1961, 1989)

The Rainbow Goblins by Ul De Rico (Thames and Hudson, 1978, 1994)

What a Wonderful World by George David Weiss and Bob Thiele (Simon & Schuster, 1995)

How About a Hug?

Purpose: To provide a writing experience and a large group shared literature extension that can be presented as a valentine.

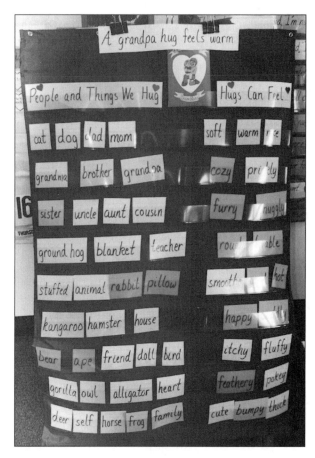

 Materials

- 34″ x 42″ pocket chart
- *A Book of Hugs*, by Dave Ross (HarperCollins, 1980)
- Marker
- Scissors
- Glue
- About 20 tag quality sentence strips or end pieces (10 each in two different colors)
- Heart pattern (See page 31.)
- 24″ x 36″ sheet of red construction paper cut in half width-wise to make two pieces of 12″ x 36″ paper. (You can fold paper inward in half and then half again and then place the heart pattern along the fold. Trace and cut one heart-shaped accordion book from each half. Be careful not to cut the folded edge. If this paper is unavailable, craft paper from rolls can be cut to size. Then children can color the hearts as desired.)
- Manuscript paper (Cut to shape or decrease the size of the heart pattern by about 1/2-inch all around. Then trace it onto manuscript paper. Draw two lines for writing across the top and make four copies per child.)

Pocket Chart Words

- **People and Things We Hug**
- **Hugs Can Feel**
- **words brainstormed with children**

◆ ■ ◆ Setup ◆ ■ ◆

1. Read *A Book of Hugs* or see *Literature Integrations* for other books.

2. Explain to children that you are writing special valentines or books about loving.

3. Place each sentence strip in the pocket chart and brainstorm with children words that fit under each category. Write the words as you brainstorm and then place them in the chart.

4. Give each child four pieces of the heart-shaped paper on which to write their sentences and illustrations about hugs using the frame: A _____ hug feels _____. For example: A dog hug feels furry. Encourage them to use words from the pocket chart.

5. When children complete their writing and illustrations, have them cut out the hearts and glue them onto accordion heart books.

◆ ■ ◆ Variations ◆ ■ ◆

1. Create a class big book of hugs using paper cut into large hearts. Your class can choose its favorite hugs from the chart to illustrate.

2. Create a class mural of hugs. Glue sentence strips and corresponding illustrations onto mural paper or onto large hearts and then display them on a bulletin board.

◆ ■ ◆ Literature Integrations ◆ ■ ◆

The Mysterious Valentine by Nancy Carlson (Penguin, 1985)

Things to Make and Do for Valentine's Day by Tomie de Paola (Franklin Watts, 1967)

Will You Be My Valentine? by Steven Kroll (Holiday House Inc., 1993)

Babushka Baba Yaga by Patricia Polacco (The Putnam Grosset Group, 1993)

Valentine Friends by Ann Schweninger (Penguin, 1988)

Loving by Ann Morris (William Morrow & Co., 1990)

CHAPTER TWO

Pocket Charts for Special Days and Seasons

Recognizing seasonal changes and special days with a pocket chart tradition in your classroom can add to the understanding and excitement of these events.

Apple Tree

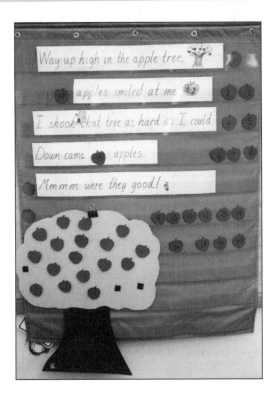

Purpose: To teach counting and introduce addition and subtraction through learning and reciting a simple poem about a favorite fall fruit.

Materials

- 34" x 42" pocket chart
- 6 white tag quality sentence strips
- Red, black and green permanent markers
- 2 22" x 28" sheets of 4- or 6-ply red tagboard
- 1 22" x 28" sheet of 4- or 6-ply brown tagboard
- 1 22" x 28" sheet of 4- or 6-ply green tagboard
- Scissors
- Easel clip
- 12-inch self-adhesive Velcro
- Apple pattern (See page 37.)
- Tree pattern (See pages 36-37.)
- Tacky glue

Pocket Chart Words

Way up high in the apple tree,
____ apples smiled at me.
I shook that tree as hard as I could.
Down came ____ apples.
Mmmm were they good!

◆ ■ ◼ Setup ◆ ■ ◼

1. Write the poem on sentence strips with either a red or green marker.

2. Using the pattern, trace and then cut out apples. The number you cut will depend on what number you'd like to count up to.(If you're counting up to 20, you'll need 30 apples.)

3. Using the pattern, trace and then cut out the tree top from green tagboard.

4. Using the pattern, trace and then cut out the tree trunk from brown tagboard.

5. Glue the tree top to the tree trunk.

6. Cut Velcro into small pieces and attach one side of the Velcro onto the apples and attach other side onto the tree top.

7. With black permanent marker number the apples 1 to 20 and then number the remaining apples 1 to 10. One set of numbered apples can be placed in the poem, and the other set can be used to complete the equation.

8. Place the poem and some apples in the pocket chart. Use an easel clip to hang the tree on the pocket chart. You and your children can change the numbers of apples in the poem for practice in counting, adding and subtracting.

◆ ■ ◼ Variations ◆ ■ ◼

1. Teach the poem from the chart and then set it up as an independent learning center.

2. Have children pretend to be the apples falling off the tree, matching the number on the tree.

3. You can write equations on chart paper as the class changes the numbers in the pocket chart.

4. Children write the equations as the class changes the numbers in the poem.

◆ ■ ◼ Literature Integrations ◆ ■ ◼

The Story of Johnny Appleseed by Aliki (Simon & Schuster for Young Readers, 1963)

The Seasons of Arnold's Apple Tree by Gail Gibbons (Harcourt Brace Jovanovich, 1984)

Picking Apples and Pumpkins by Amy and Richard Hutchings (Scholastic, 1994)

How Do Apples Grow? by Betsy Maestro (HarperCollins, 1992)

Five Sparkling Snowmen

Purpose: To learn about or reinforce winter vocabulary, to cite attributes of seasonal changes and to contrast winter and spring while reciting and performing a finger play about snowmen.

 **Materials**

- Sentence strips in two different colors
- Snowy decorations like stickers or a border

Hint: Holiday cards often depict snowy scenes.
- Snowmen or snow people drawn or cut from displays

Pocket Chart Words

"Five Sparkling Snowmen"
poem by Valerie SchifferDanoff

Five sparkling snowmen
Watching children play
The first one said, "How long can we
stay?"
The second one said, "Until the
temperature climbs."
The third one said, "In winter we have
good times."
The fourth one said, "I wish we'd last
all year"
The fifth one said, "We leave when
spring is here."

Setup

1. Write the narrative on sentence strips in one color.

2. Write the speaking parts on sentence strips in another color.

3. Place sentence strips and snow people decorations in pocket chart.

4. Read the poem chorally with children and then allow them to take turns playing each part.

Science/Math Connection

If it is winter and it has been snowing where you live, bring some snow inside. Have children guess or estimate how long it will take for the snow to melt. Once the snow melts, compare the volume to that of the snow. Then see how many days it takes for the water to evaporate.

Literature Integrations

Sadie and the Snowman by Allen Morgan (Kids Can Press, 1985)

Bob the Snowman by Sylvia Loretan (Penguin, 1988)

The Mystery of the Missing Red Mitten by Steven Kellogg (Dial Books for Young Children, 1974)

Poetry Integrations

"Snowfall" by Margaret Hillert from *Poetry Place Anthology* (Scholastic, 1983)

"I Built a Little Snowman" author unknown from *The Scholastic Integrated Language Arts Resource Book* (Scholastic, 1995)

My Kite

Purpose: To recognize activities and weather changes associated with spring. To recognize rhyming and spelling patterns as in *kite, flight, tight, bright* and *sight*. To teach the "ing" suffix and to help students see that while another "n" is added to run for running, it is not added to shine but rather the "e" is dropped.

 Materials

- 7 tag quality sentence strips in different colors
- Kite stickers or kite pictures
- Kite pattern (See page 42.)
- Fadeless art tagboard
- Markers
- Scissors
- String, ribbon or construction paper

Pocket Chart Words

"My Kite"
poem by Valerie SchifferDanoff

I'm running with my kite.
I'm holding the string tight.
It's sailing high in flight.
It's flying through the light.
In shining sun so bright.
It's going out of sight.

 Setup

1. Write each line of the poem on a sentence strip in a different color. If you have kite stickers, place one on each sentence strip.

2. Trace the pattern and cut out kites or have children draw kites for the display.

3. Children can attach string, ribbon or a strip of construction paper to make tails.

Variations

1. Children can copy the poem for handwriting.

2. Each child can create his or her own kite on a sheet of 12" x 18" drawing paper and attach the poem to the kite shape.

3. Children can write about kite-flying experiences.

4. Children can fly a kite outside.

5. Children can learn the poem and recite it chorally.

6. Children can set the words to hand, eye, feet and body motions.

Science Connection

Discuss and experiment with other wind-powered objects, like small paper sail boats in water. This can be done inside the classroom with a container of water and a fan or by the power of breathing, or outside in a body of water with wind.

Literature Integrations

Catch the Wind! All About Kites by Gail Gibbons (Little Brown & Co., 1989)

Kites by Bettina Ling (Scholastic, 1994)

The Wind Blew by Pat Hutchins (Macmillan, 1974)

Gilberto and the Wind by Marie Hall Ets (Penguin, 1963)

Mirandy and Brother Wind by Patricia C. McKissack (Alfred Knopf, 1988)

The Emperor and the Kite by Jane Yolen (The Putnam Grosset Group, 1967)

Wind by Ron Bacon (Ashton Scholastic, 1984)

How the Wind Plays by Michael Lipson (Hyperion Books for Children, 1994)

Poetry Integrations

"Wouldn't You?" by John Ciardi and "A Kite" (author unknown) from *Read A-Loud Rhymes for the Very Young* selected by Jack Prelutsky (Alfred A. Knopf, 1986)

My Kite

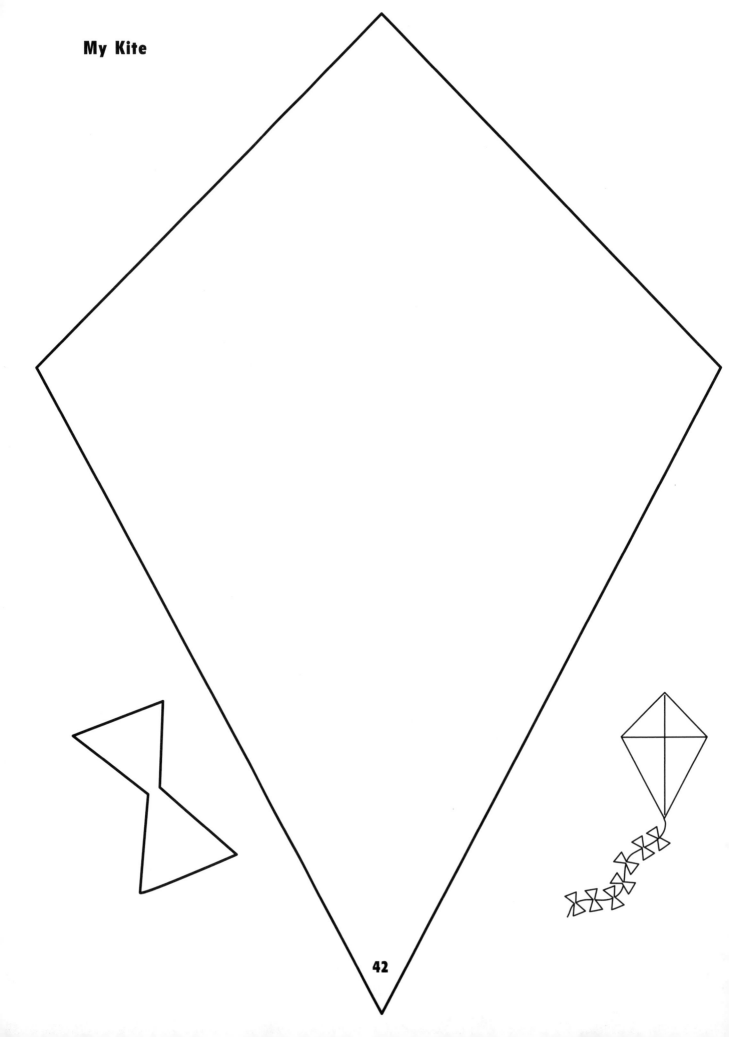

42

Five White Tail Deer

Purpose: To learn a poem for dramatic play, to share and further the understanding of traditional family holiday celebrations and to encourage discussions about how holidays are celebrated at home.

Materials

- 12 tag quality sentence strips in 2-3 different colors
- Heavy brown paper
- Deer patterns (See pages 45-46.)

- Stickers, stars, border
- Markers
- Scissors

Pocket Chart Words

"Five White Tail Deer"
poem by Valerie SchifferDanoff

Five white tail deer stood
   outside a house.
Each one quiet as a mouse.
The doe said, "That dreidel can
   really spin!"
The buck said, "I wonder who
   will win!"
One fawn said, "I see a sled going by."
The second fawn said, " Wow, it's
   really flying high!"
The third fawn said, "It's that time
   of year!"
As a child came to see,
Into the night ran the deer.

 ## Setup

1. Write the narrator parts on sentence strips in one color. Write the speaking deer parts on strips in another color.

2. Trace the deer patterns and cut them out or have children draw their own deer for the display.

3. Use stickers, stars and a border as decorations.

Literature Integrations

Tree of Cranes by Allen Say (Houghton Mifflin, 1991)

Someday by Charlotte Zolotow (Harper & Row, 1965)

Light the Lights A Story About Celebrating Hanukkah & Christmas by Margaret Moorman (Scholastic, 1994)

Mrs. Santa Claus by Penny Ives (Delecorte Press, 1990)

Hanukkah by Roni Schotter (Little Brown and Co., 1990)

Too Many Tamales by Gary Soto (The Putnam Grosset Group, 1993)

Thank You Santa by Margaret Wild (Ashton Scholastic, 1991)

Deer at the Brook by Jim Arnosky (William Morrow, 1986)

buck

Five White Tail Deer

Cut 2.

doe

Friends Are Special

Purpose: To learn a poem and encourage a feeling of friendship and thankfulness which can broaden the meaning and understanding of Thanksgiving.

Materials

- 34" x 42" pocket chart
- 5 yellow and 6 orange sentence strips
- Drawing paper
- Markers
- Crayons
- Scissors

Pocket Chart Words

"Friends Are Special"
poem by Valerie SchifferDanoff

Five little children on a special day,
All of them thankful in their own way.
The first one said, "I love my family!"
The second one said, "I'm thankful for
　every tree!"
The third one said, "I'm thankful
　we're all friends!"
The fourth one said, "Friendship
　never ends!"
The fifth one said, "I'm thankful
　we all care!
And can play together year after year!"

Setup

1. Write the narrator parts on yellow
sentence strips.

2. Write the speaking parts on orange
sentence strips.

3. Read the poem with children. As
they learn the poem, children can
take turns acting out the parts and
narrating.

4. Have children draw self portraits
and cut them out. Encourage children to write their own reasons for
being thankful on their self portraits
to make a display.

Literature Integrations

The Greatest Table by Michael J. Rosen
(Harcourt Brace, 1994)

Everybody Cooks Rice by Norah Dooley
(Carolrhoda Books, 1991)

I Love My Family by Wade Hudson
(Scholastic, 1993)

*How Many Days to America? A
Thanksgiving Story* by Eve Bunting
(Houghton Mifflin, 1988)

Tikvah Means Hope by Patricia Polacco
(Bantam Doubleday, 1994)

Birthdays

Purpose: To create birthday cake books filled with children's special greetings to a child whose birthday is being celebrated.

Materials

- 24″ x 24″ or 34″ x 42″ pocket chart
- 7-10 tag quality sentence strips
- Permanent marker
- Scissors
- Glue
- Precut gummed shapes (See the *Introduction*, Pocket Chart Supplies and Sources.)
- Birthday cake and candle patterns (See page 51.)
- 12″ x 18″ sheet of construction paper in white, brown, pink or yellow (1 per child)
- Glitter writer (See the *Introduction*, Pocket Chart Supplies and Sources.)
- 6″ x 6″ assorted pieces of construction paper (1 per child)
- Manuscript paper or copy of cake pattern (See page 51.)

Pocket Chart Words

(The following are examples of children's greetings.)

Dear
Happy Birthday! Enjoy your day!
Have a wonderful day!
It's your birthday all day.
I hope you like your presents.
I hope all your wishes come true!
    From

# Setup

1. Trace the birthday cake pattern on construction paper and cut out two cake shapes for each child in your class. These will be the front and back covers of the birthday books. You may wish to fold the construction paper in half and cut two cake shapes at a time.

2. Use a glitter writer or glitter and glue to write "Happy Birthday _____!" on the front cover. Do this the day before so the glue is dry enough for the birthday child to decorate the cover with candles and stick-on shapes.

3. Use the cake pattern to precut manuscript paper into cake shapes. The amount will depend on the number of students in your class. Each time your class celebrates a birthday, you'll need one sheet of cake-shaped manuscript paper per child in your class to complete the book. Allow one for yourself too. *Note:* Parent volunteers can help keep up your supply or cake-shaped paper.

4. Trace the candle patterns onto construction paper. The birthday child can cut these out while the other children are writing their greetings. If you are teaching kindergarten, the candles will need to be precut.

5. When assembling the books you may want to include a copy of the birthday song or the following birthday poem.

This little birthday cake,
Decorated for me
Has _____ candles on the top
For everyone to see.

When I have a party,
This is what I'll do—
I'll make a wish and blow real hard
And hope my wish comes true.

6. Write birthday greetings on sentence strips for the children to copy.

7. Place the sentence strips, the back and front covers and the manuscript paper cakes in the pocket chart so children can help themselves.

Literature Integrations

Happy Birthday A Pop-up Treasury of World Birthday Legend and Lore by Joan Bowden (Houghton Mifflin, 1994)

Happy Birthday, Moon by Frank Asch (Prentice-Hall, 1982)

The Birthday Moon by Lois Duncan (Penguin, 1989)

Hello, Amigos! by Tricia Brown (Henry Holt, 1986)

Some Birthday! by Patricia Polacco (Simon & Schuster, 1991)

Mouse's Birthday by Jane Yolen (The Putnam & Grosset Group, 1993)

Birthdays

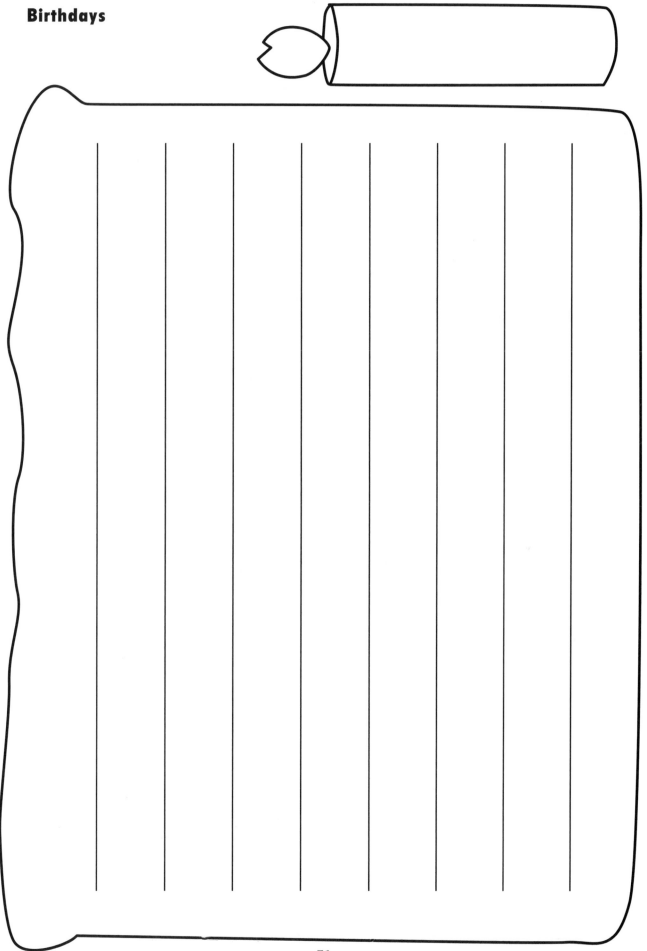

Special Person Profile

Purpose: To build pride and understanding by presenting information about oneself using a pocket chart.

One last special day pocket chart you might like to try in your classroom gives every child a chance to be the star for a day. Children can use it to tell about their life outside of school, in school or both. The day could coincide with the completion of a special project or school published book.

 **Materials**

- 34" x 42" pocket chart
- 10 tag quality sentence strips
- Photos, drawings, small trinkets

Pocket Chart Words

• These will depend on what the child chooses to tell about herself or himself.

Setup

1. Tell children that they will each have the opportunity to present a pocket-chart profile for a day.

2. Work out a schedule. It could coincide with birthdays, but it doesn't have to.

3. About one week before a child's day, have the child write his or her ten sentences in a writing journal. In the case of younger children, skip this step and have the child dictate sentences to you.

4. Two days before the designated day, have the child copy the sentences onto sentence strips. Give assistance as needed.

5. The day before, have the child gather any items that he or she would like displayed in or near the pocket chart.

6. On the pocket-chart profile day, the child can set up the pocket chart and present it to the class. The chart can remain up for a day. Pictured on page 52 is mine, "About the Author." You may want to start the tradition in your classroom by presenting one about yourself, titled "About Your Teacher."

Literature Integrations

Chrysanthemum by Kevin Henkes (William Morrow, 1991)

Quick as a Cricket by Audrey Wood (Child's Play, 1982)

Cleversticks by Bernard Stokley (HarperCollins, 1991)

Soapsuds and Other Verses by Karla Kuskin (HarperCollins, 1952)

What Do You Like? by Michael Grejniec (North South Books, 1992)

Wilfred Gordon McDonald Partridge by Mem Fox (Kane Miller Books, 1985)

CHAPTER THREE

Pocket Charts for Making Things

Children enjoy these independent activities that result in a completed project. Pocket charts can create a center for a greeting card company or publishing company, an art center or even a restaurant.

Creating Greeting Cards

Purpose: To follow directions to complete an independent writing activity— making a greeting card for a friend or family member.

 Materials

- 2 34″ x 42″ pocket charts
- 20 tag qualilty sentence strips
- Scissors (for teacher and child)
- Shape patterns (See page 58.)
- Tagboard to make templates
- Permanent marker
- Envelopes
- Drawing paper cut so that when folded it will fit in envelopes (Just double the width of the envelope, measure the same length.)
- Markers, crayons and glue
- Wrapping paper (from which children can create cards)
- Greeting cards for samples

Pocket Chart Words

(Pocket chart 1)

1. Fold the paper in half.
2. Check to see if the paper fits in the envelope.
3. Open the card like a book.
4. Write Dear _____ or To _____,
5. Write the message.
6. Write Love, or From, "You," Your name.
7. Decorate your cards carefully.
8. Write the name on the envelope.

(Pocket chart 2)

To whom can I write my card?

People: dad, mom, sister, brother, uncle, aunt, friend, teacher, principal, granddad, grandma, cousin

Special Days: birthday, holiday, Christmas, Hanukkah, communion, Bar Mitzvah, Bat Mitzvah, anniversary, Kwanzaa, New Year's, Valentine's Day, Easter

Greetings: happy, best, very, great, wishes, congratulations, thank you, much, welcome, merry, Feliz Navidad, Feliz Cumpleaños, Omedeto, Gung Hoy Fat Choy!

These words are placed in the pocket chart for children: heart, star, teddy bear, circle, candle, tree. This will help children return the templates to their appropriate spaces. It also helps children learn new words and spelling.

 **Setup**

1. Write the directions for making a card on sentence strips and place them in pocket chart 1. Keeping a small book and envelopes nearby will help children to remember how to fold the card and to check it for correct fit.

2. Brainstorm with children or prewrite message words on sentence strips. Place them in pocket chart 2. Write each set of words on sentence strips in one color. For example, write all "people" words on blue sentence strips.

3. Trace the shape patterns onto tagboard to make templates. Place these in pocket chart 2 also.

4. Place precut paper, wrapping paper (you can ask children to bring this to school), crayons, markers, scissors and glue on a table near the pocket charts.

5. Pair children and give a full-class lesson on how to make a card by having each child make a card for his or her friend.

This activity can highlight cultural traditions and celebrations throughout the year.

Literature Integrations

The Jolly Postman and Other People's Letters by Janet and Allan Ahlberg (William Heinemann Ltd., 1986)

Thank You Santa by Margaret Wild (Omnibus Books, 1991)

Hanukkah by Roni Schotter (Joy Street Books, 1990)

My First Kwanzaa Book by Deborah M. Chocolate Newton (Scholastic, 1992)

Valentine Friends by Ann Schweninger (Penguin, 1988)

(See also *Literature Integrations* for the Birthday Cake page 50.)

A Snack for New Friends

Purpose: To practice following directions and to strengthen small motor skills, children spread peanut butter or cream cheese on a rice cake and continue placing other food items on top to create a face. This is a good way to break the ice at the beginning of the school year.

◆ ■ ■ Materials ◆ ■ ■

- 24″ x 24″ pocket chart
- 7 tag quality sentence strips
- Rice cakes, mini marshmallows, raisins, sliced apples, shredded carrot, peanut butter and cream cheese (amounts will depend on the number of children in your class)
- Plastic knives
- Paper plates

Pocket Chart Words

Make a new friend

1. Spread peanut butter or cream cheese on a rice cake.
2. Give your friend raisin eyes, a marshmallow nose and an apple smile.
3. Put some shredded carrot on for hair.

Enjoy your friend with a friend.

 Setup

1. Write the pocket chart words on sentence strips and place them in the pocket chart.

2. Prepare enough ingredients for each child in your class. Place these on a table near the pocket chart along with paper plates and plastic knives.

3. Model the directions with children.

4. Once everybody has completed their friendly snack, children can trade with a friend or eat their own.

Variations

1. Have a silent preparation. Arrange ingredients for each child on tables in your classroom. Then have everyone read and follow the directions silently themselves. Once complete, everyone can eat!

2. Try other simple snack directions. For example, children can make a rabbit by using two carrot sticks for ears and celery sticks for whiskers.

3. Celebrate holidays and family traditions with a special snack.

4. Set up this activity as a restaurant center during the year. It provides an independent activity that calls for a lot of will power too!

Literature Integrations

Rabbit Mooncakes by Hoong Yee Lee Krakauer (Little Brown & Co, 1994)

Many Friends Cooking cooked and written by Terry Touff Cooper and Marilyn Ratner (Philomel Books, 1980)

1000 Silly Sandwiches by Alan Benjamin (Simon & Schuster, 1995)

School Days by B.G. Hennessy (Penguin, 1990)

Yo Yes! by Chris Raschka (Orchard Books, 1993)

Puffins for a "Puffinry"

Purpose: To learn how to follow directions and to develop fine motor skills through tracing, cutting and gluing puffin parts together to make a paper puffin.

Materials

- 34″ x 42″ pocket chart
- 6 sentence strips
- Permanent markers (for teacher)
- Markers or crayons, pencils (for children)
- Scissors (for children and teacher)
- Glue (for children and teacher)
- Puffin parts patterns (See pages 63-65.)
- Tagboard to make puffin templates

- 12″ x 18″ sheet of black construction paper (1 per child and 1 for your model)
- 9″ x 12″ sheet of white construction paper (1 per child and 1 for your model)
- 4″ x 4″ pieces of yellow and orange construction paper (1 per child and 1 for your model)

Pocket Chart Words

A Puffin can walk, fly, swim and dive.

1. Trace and cut the puffin's body.
2. Trace and cut the puffin's face and beak.
3. Trace and cut the puffin's white feathers.
4. Trace and cut the puffin's feet.
5. Glue your puffin together.

Setup

1. Trace patterns and cut out templates for puffin parts.

2. Fabricate puffins from the templates to use as models.

3. Write the puffin directions on sentence strips.

4. Place the directions and templates in the pocket chart. Place the other materials nearby.

5. Read about puffins and show children pictures of real puffins. (See *Literature Integrations* below.)

6. Read the directions in the pocket chart before children begin.
Note: A real puffin is 12 inches tall.

7. Mount the puffins on paper in a different color and display them together so your class can have their own puffinry and have fun learning about this interesting bird nicknamed, "clown of the sea."

Poetry Integrations

"There once was a puffin" by Florence Page Jacque (See page 25.)

"The Puffin" by Robert Williams Wood, from *The Random House Book of Poetry* (Random House, 1983)

Literature Integrations

Baby Beluga by Raffi (Crown, 1983)

Puffin's Homecoming The Story of an Atlantic Puffin by Darice Bailer (Trudy Management Corporation, 1993)

The Puffins are Back! by Gail Gibbons (HarperCollins, 1991)

Puffin 1

63

Puffin 2

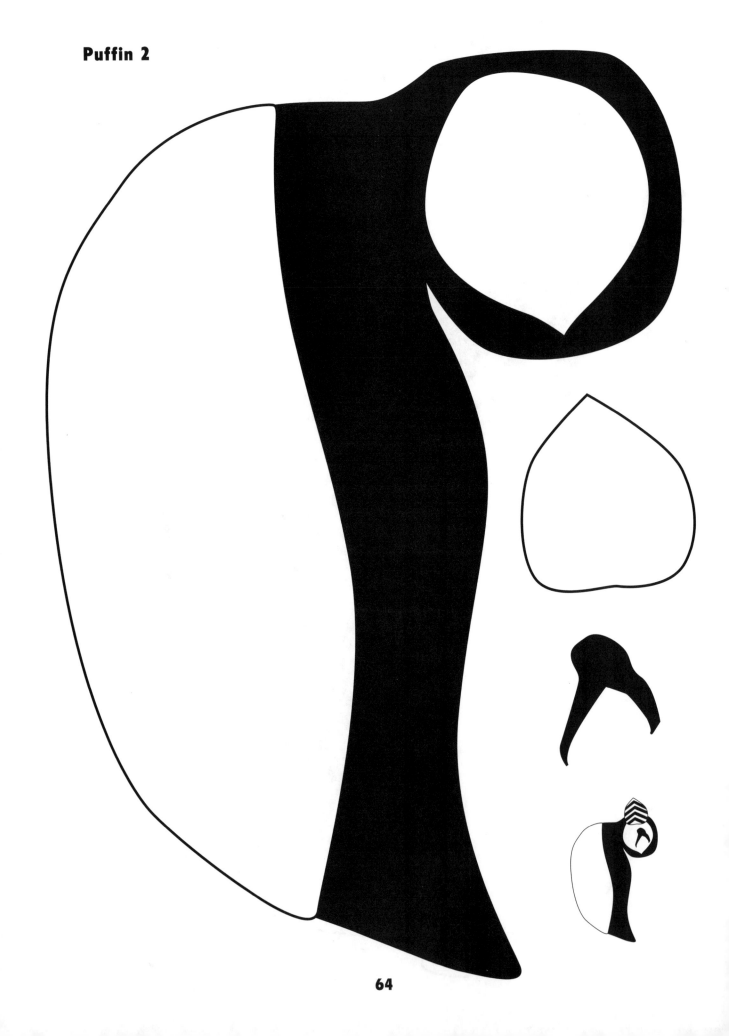

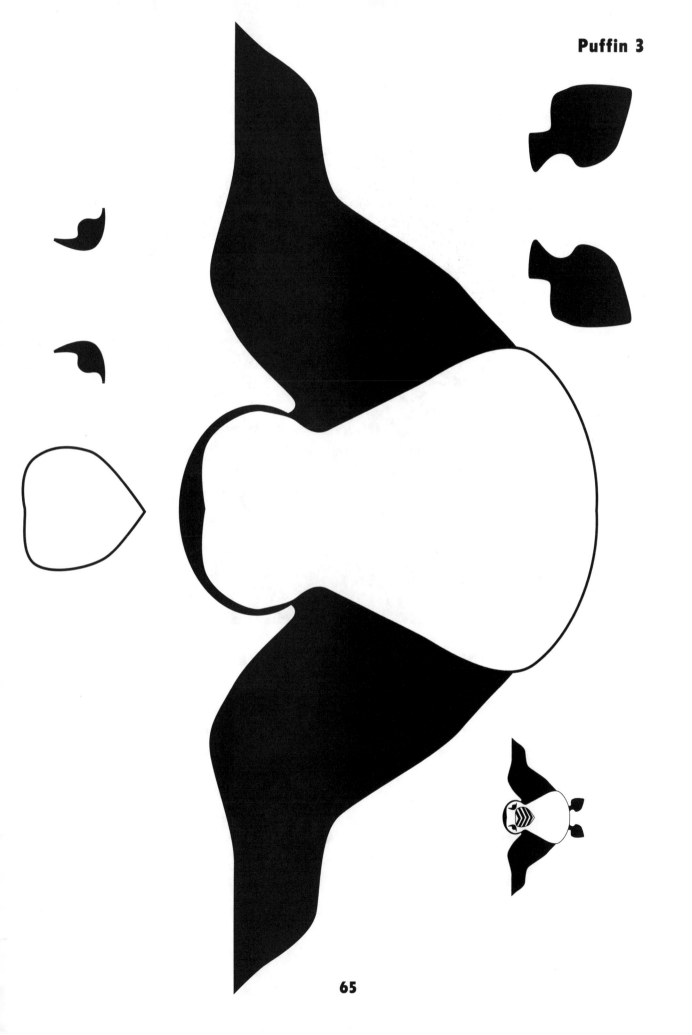

A Tooth Shape Book

Purpose: To research clues for an independent writing activity in which a "guess who" book about animals, their missing teeth and their habitats is created.

◆ ◆ ◆ Materials ◆ ◆ ◆

- 34″ x 42″ pocket chart
- 8 sentence strips
- Permanent markers (for teacher)
- Markers and crayons (for children)
- Scissors (for teacher and children)
- Glue (for teacher and children)
- Tooth patterns (See page 68.)
- Tagboard for tooth templates
- 12″ x 18″ sheets of white construction paper (3-4 per child)
- Copies of bubble page (See page 69.)
- Stapler

Pocket Chart Words

Who lost a tooth?

1. Trace and cut large and small teeth.
2. Draw an animal on each tooth page.
3. Glue just the top edge of the small tooth to cover each animal.
4. Write animal clues on bubbles. Glue bubble clues to each page. Staple your tooth book together.

Setup

1. Trace the tooth pattern onto tagboard to make tooth templates.

2. Create a sample book. One page might look and read as follows: On the bubble write the clue: "I love to eat the tulips in your garden. I am a vegetarian." On the tooth page draw a deer and then make a lift-flap by gluing the upper edge of the smaller tooth to cover the picture on the rest of the page. Draw a forest scene and then glue the bubble near the small tooth.

3. Write the pocket chart directions.

4. Copy the bubble page for each child.

5. Place the directions, your sample and the templates in the pocket chart. Place other materials nearby.

6. Read over the directions with children. Encourage them to consult books about animals for ideas. See *Literature Integrations* for possible selections.

Literature Integrations

Little Rabbit's Loose Tooth by Lucy Bate (Scholastic, 1975)

Loose Tooth by Steven Kroll (Holiday House, 1984)

What Big Teeth You Have by Patricia Lauber (HarperCollins, 1986)

Animals in the Wild Series (Raintree Publishers)

How Many Teeth? by Paul Showers (HarperCollins, 1991)

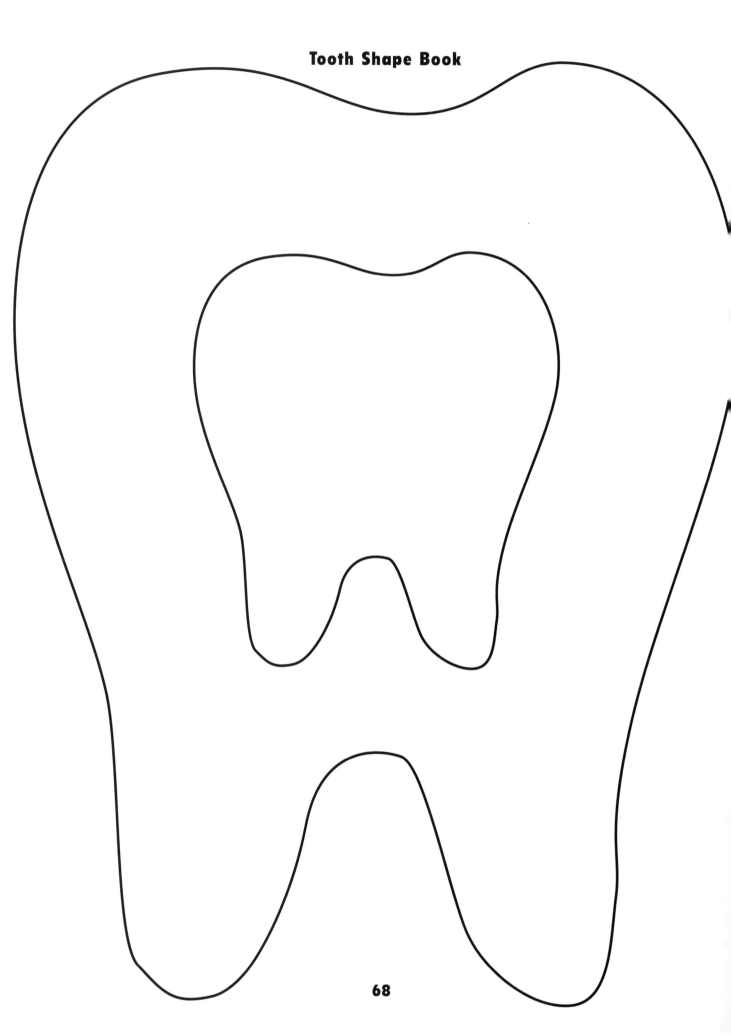

A Rabbit Slide-Up

Purpose: To do an independent art and writing activity, creating an illustration, poem and a slide-up rabbit.

Materials

- 34" x 42" pocket chart
- 9 tag quality sentence strips
- Permanent markers
- Scissors (teacher and student)
- Markers, crayons, glue (for teacher and student)
- Rabbit and flower-pot patterns (See page 72.)
- Tagboard for templates and rabbit slide

1 of the following for each child and your model:

- 12" x 18" sheet of pale blue construction paper
- 9" x 12" sheet of green construction paper
- 6" x 6" piece of brown, black or white construction paper for the rabbit
- 6" x 6" piece of red construction paper for the pot

Pocket Chart Words

Where is the rabbit?

1. Trace and cut a rabbit.
2. Trace and cut a flower pot.
3. Glue the rabbit to the slide stick.
4. Fringe green paper for grass. Glue the green paper to the blue background paper.
5. Draw flowers.
6. Write a rabbit poem or story. I'll help you put the slide-up together.

 Setup

1. Trace the patterns onto tagboard to make templates and then make a model of the rabbit and slide for demonstration.

2. Write the pocket chart directions on sentence strips. Draw small illustrations on sentence strips. (See photograph on page 70.)

3. Place templates, sentence strips and 1" x 8" pieces of tagboard (for slide) in the pocket chart, and then place the other supplies nearby.

4. Demonstrate to children how the slide works as you go over the directions in the pocket chart. Younger children will need some help putting the slide-up together.

Variation

Write a rabbit poem and place it in another pocket chart nearby. Invite children to copy the poem onto paper which can be glued onto the grass. You might like to try this poem that has been passed from teacher to teacher:

Here is a bunny,
With ears so funny!
Here is his hole in the ground.
When a noise he hears,
He picks up his ears.
And hops into his hole in the ground.

Literature Integrations

The Tale of Rabbit and Coyote by Tony Johnston (Putnam and Grosset Group, 1994)

Little Rabbit Foo Foo retold by Michael Rosen (Simon & Schuster, 1990)

Pop-up Baby Bunny by Peggy Tagel (Putnam Grosset Book Group, 1991)

Marshmallow by Claire Turlay Newberry (HarperCollins, 1942, 1970)

The Rabbit Story by Alvin Tresselt (William Morrow, 1957, 1989)

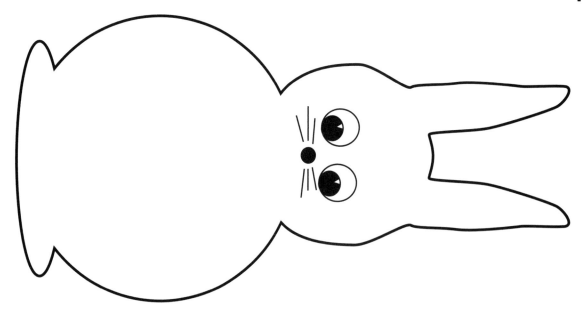

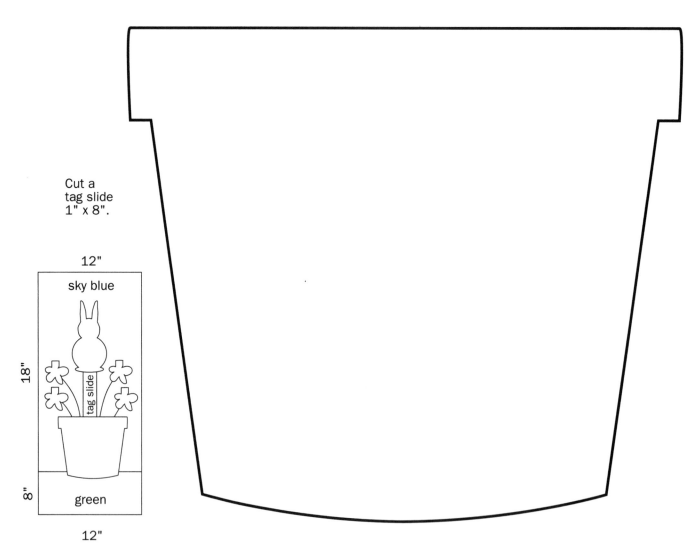

Cut a
tag slide
1" x 8".

12"

sky blue

18"

tag slide

8"

green

12"

Pocket Charts
for Math

Pocket charts for math provide you and the children with
another manipulative hands-on format for learning math
concepts. These can be set up as a literature extension, a
follow-up to a math lesson or as part of a theme center.

Recipe for a Pattern

Purpose: To identify and count items to create patterns.

◆ ▪ ◇ Materials ◆ ▪ ◇

- 24″ x 24″ pocket chart
- 6 tag quality sentence strips in 2-3 different colors
- Small plastic toys or place stickers or drawings on tag-quality
- Plastic bowl (to hold items)
- Smaller plastic dish (for children to place items once chosen so that more than one child can work with the chart at a time)

Note: Try to acquire some toys because that is what makes this center all the more attractive. Whatever you use, have about 20 of each item on hand. Inexpensive, small plastic toys are available in party shops or see the Introduction, Pocket Chart Supplies and Sources.

Pocket Chart Words

Creature Cafe Stew
Recipe for a Pattern
(numbers)
(item names)
(These will mostly depend on the small plastic toys or stickers on tagboard that you have gathered. The chart shown is keyed into a Halloween theme. However, for a regular restaurant-type theme, try miniature fruits and vegetables which are available through catalogs and at craft stores.)

 **Setup**

1. Write the numbers 1 to 20 on sentence strips in one color so that the amounts can be changed. You may want to make doubles of some numbers in order to create certain number patterns (see the photograph).

2. Write item names on sentence strips in another color. You can vary these too.

3. You can write the name of the recipe on a sentence strip in a third color.

4. Place the numbers and item names in the pocket chart.

5. Place the bowl with the items in it and the plate near the pocket chart.

Variation

Try a fruit salad or a vegetable soup recipe. Use vegetable or fruit math manipulatives purchased from a catalog like ETA (1-800-445-5985).

Literature Integrations

One Hungry Monster A Counting Book in Rhyme by Susan Heyboer O'Keefe (Little Brown, 1989)

The Hungry Thing Goes to a Restaurant by Jan Slepian and Ann Seidler (Scholastic, 1992)

Little Witch's Book of Magic Spells by Deborah Hautzig (Random House, 1988)

Stone Soup by Ann McGovern (Scholastic, 1986)

Growing Vegetable Soup by Lois Ehlert (Harcourt Brace Jovanovich, 1987)

Eating the Alphabet by Lois Ehlert (Harcourt Brace Jovanovich, 1989)

Story Problems

Purpose: To introduce story problems about addition and subtraction, and to have children apply story-problem language while working independently or in pairs.

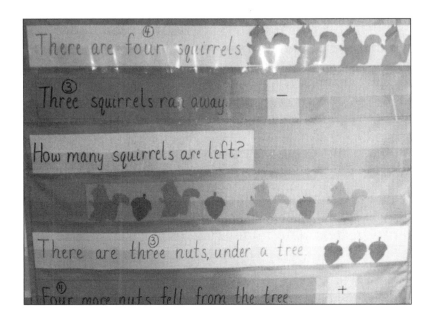

Materials

- 34″ x 42″ pocket chart
- Sentence strips in 4 different colors (Amount you'll need of each will vary depending on how many different problems you want to write. The problems in the pocket chart can be changed daily or every other day.)
- Permanent markers
- Squirrel and nut patterns (See page 77.)
- Gray and brown tagboard for squirrels and nuts
- Scissors

Pocket Chart Words

There are four squirrels.
Three squirrels ran away.
How many squirrels are left?
-   +
There are three nuts under a tree.
Four more nuts fell from the tree.
How many nuts are there all together?
(2 sets of numbers 1-9)

1. Write each sentence of the story problem on a sentence strip in a different color.

2. Write the numbers and operations on sentence strips in different colors.

3. Trace the squirrel and nut patterns onto tagboard and cut them out. You may wish to make ten of each.

4. Place the story problems, numbers, squirrels and nuts in the chart. Be sure to hang the pocket chart at a height children can reach.

5. Read the pocket chart with children showing them how to move the pieces as needed.

Children can copy the story problem and illustrate it after they've moved the squirrels to complete the equations for the correct answers.

Literature Integrations

12 Ways to Get to 11 by Eve Merriam (Simon & Schuster, 1993)

Squirrels by Brian Wildsmith (Oxford University Press, 1974)

Red Leaf, Yellow Leaf by Lois Ehlert (Harcourt Brace Jovanovich, 1989)

Nuts to You! by Lois Ehlert (Harcourt Brace Jovanovich, 1993)

Comparison Chart

Purpose: To chart two inquiries so that information can be gathered, shared, counted and compared.

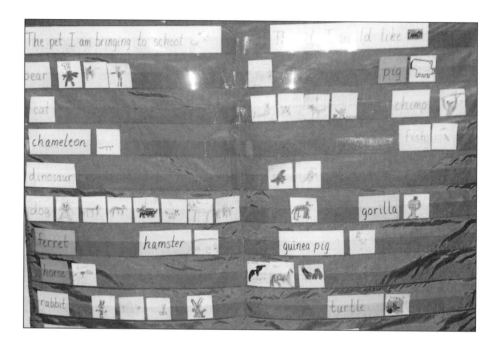

 Materials

- 2 34" x 42" or 1 58" x 42" pocket chart (pictured)
- 2 tag quality sentence strips
- Sentence strip pieces
- 3" x 3" pieces of white drawing paper
- Permanent marker
- Crayons (for children)

Pocket Chart Words

The pocket chart pictured above compares pets children are bringing to school, which include stuffed animals, to pets children have and would like to have. It reads as follows:

The pet I am bringing to school.
The pet I would like.

(These words came from children's suggestions: bear, cat, chameleon, dinosaur, dog, ferret, hamster, horse, rabbit, seal, tiger, pig, chimp, fish, gorilla, guinea pig, turtle, alligator.)

◆ ■ ◆ Setup ◆ ■ ◆

1. Write the sentences about pets on the sentence strips.

2. Brainstorm possibilities for pets with your class. Write these on the sentence strip pieces. Have children appropriately place them in the pocket chart.

3. Give each child two pieces of drawing paper on which to draw a response to each sentence. Children place these in the pocket chart when complete.

4. After the responses are in complete view, count and compare them with children. You'll also have a record as to what animals will be brought to school.

◆ ■ ◆ Variations ◆ ■ ◆

You can create a comparison pocket chart about a variety of subjects. Some teachers like to create one pocket chart per week as part of their math program. Here are some ideas.

- What did you bring for snack today? What do you wish you had for snack?

- What did you eat for dinner last night? What are you hoping for tonight?

- My favorite thing to read about. What I would write a book about.

- My favorite place to visit. Where I would like to live.

◆ ■ ◆ Literature Integrations ◆ ■ ◆

Oh Kojo! How could you! by Verna Aardema (Penguin, 1984)

My Painted House, My Friendly Chicken and Me by Maya Angelou (Clarkson and Potter, 1994)

Arthur's Pet Business by Marc Brown (Little Brown & Co., 1990)

I Really Want a Dog by Sally Blakemore and Susan Breslow (Penguin, 1990)

Measuring Up

Purpose: To measure items and record findings.

 **Materials**

- 34″ x 42″ or 24″ x 24″ pocket chart
- *Inch by Inch* by Leo Lionni (Astor Honor/Division of Beauty House, 1960)
- 6 tag quality sentence strips
- Permanent marker (for teacher)
- Pencils, markers, crayons
- Scissors (for children)
- 9″ x 12″ pieces of drawing paper (1 per child plus 1 for your sample)
- 12-inch worm pattern (See page 82.)
- 2″ x 12″ pieces of construction paper (1 per child plus 1 for your sample)
- 12-inch ruler

Pocket Chart Words

Twelve Inch Worm

1. Trace, cut and color a 12″ worm.
2. Draw yourself.
3. Mark lines from your body.
4. Measure yourself with the worm. Each of the sections is one inch.

◆ ■ ◆ Setup ◆ ■ ◆

1. Write the directions on sentence strips and place them in the pocket chart.

2. Trace the worm pattern to make a template.

3. Make a worm and then draw a picture of yourself. Add these to the pocket chart.

4. Read the book *Inch by Inch* to the class. Discuss what else can be measured. Show a real ruler and compare it to the 12-inch worm template.

5. Go over the directions.

6. Model measuring with the worm. Show children how the "worm" can be wrapped around their wrists, for example, and how to count the "worm sections" from the point where the measure begins and ends.

◆ ■ ◆ Variations ◆ ■ ◆

1. Invite children to draw and measure other things in the classroom.

2. Children can take the 12-inch worms home to draw and measure things at home.

3. Read *Inch by Inch* and then set up the pocket chart in your classroom as an independent follow-up or literature extension for large group shared reading.

◆ ■ ◆ Poetry Integration

"Under the Ground" by Rhoda W. Bacmeister and "Only My Opinion" by Monica Shannon from *Read A-Loud Rhymes for the Very Young* selected by Jack Prelutsky (Alfred A. Knopf, 1986)

◆ ■ ◆ Literature Integrations

Worms Wiggle by David Pelham and Michael Foreman (Simon & Schuster, 1988)

Earthworm by Andrienne Soutter-Perrot (American Education Publishing, 1993)

Measuring Up

Pocket Charts From Poem to Project

Pocket charts provide an excellent space to display poetry which can be coordinated with a project extension. These charts can be displayed as a center for an independent activity or a response follow-up.

Mirror Image Butterfly

Purpose: To encourage an appreciation of poetry while providing an opportunity for artistic expression.

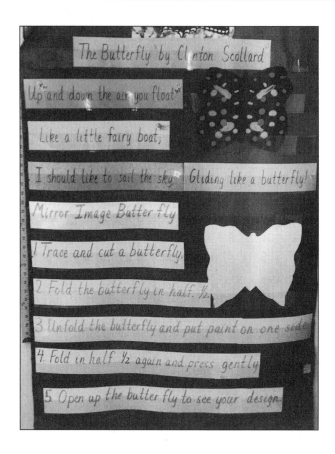

Materials

- 34" x 42" pocket chart
- 11 tag quality sentence strips
- Permanent markers (for teacher)
- Butterfly pattern (See page 86.)
- Scissors (for teacher and students)
- Photos of real butterflies from books or magazines
- Tagboard for template
- 10" x 12" sheets of black construction paper (Tru-Ray Fadeless is recommended.)
- Assorted colors of neon paint in green, pink, orange, yellow and blue
- Small recycled yogurt or cream cheese containers (to hold paint)
- Paint brushes
- Pipe cleaners
- Tape

Pocket Chart Words

"The Butterfly" by Clinton Scollard
(from *Read A-Loud Rhymes for the Very Young* selected by Jack Prelutsky, Alfred A. Knopf, 1986)

Up and down the air you float
Like a little fairy boat;
I should like to sail the sky,
Gliding like a butterfly!

Mirror Image Butterfly

1. Trace and cut a butterfly.
2. Fold the butterfly in half. 1/2
3. Unfold the butterfly and put paint on one side.
4. Fold in half 1/2 again and press gently.
5. Open up the butterfly to see your design.

You can help children by taping pipe cleaner antennae to the back of the butterfly's head when the paint is dry.

◆ ▪ ◆ Setup ◆ ▪ ◆

1. Use the pattern of the butterfly to make a template. Next write the poem and the directions on sentence strips and place them in the pocket chart.

2. Place the construction paper, paint (in containers) and paint brushes on a table near the pocket chart.

3. Read the poem with children and show pictures of butterflies if available.

4. Demonstrate for children how to apply the paint while you create your own model right in front of them.

◆ ▪ ◆ Variation ◆ ▪ ◆

Once the butterflies are complete, have each child tell you a butterfly fact. Write the facts on sentence strips. Mount the strips with the butterfly on sheets of 12" x 18" construction paper. Display their work as a class big book or create a spectacular bulletin board. Use the sentence strips from the pocket chart poem in the display too.

◆ ▪ ◆ Literature Integrations

Coyote and the Butterfly adapted by Joseph Bruchac (Scholastic, 1993)

Butterfly by Moira Butterfield (Simon & Schuster, 1991)

Discovering Butterflies by Douglas Florian (Macmillan, 1986)

I Wish I Were A Butterfly by James Howe (Harcourt Brace & Co., 1987)

Darkness and the Butterfly by Ann Grifalconi (Little Brown & Co., 1987)

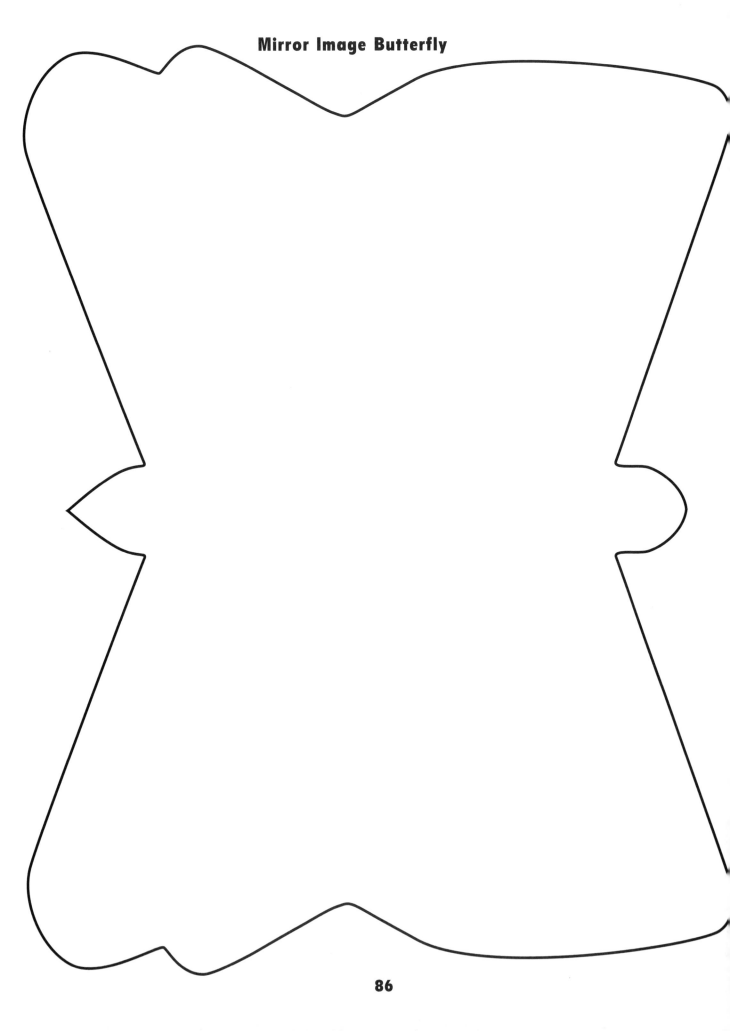

Wish for a Fish

Purpose: To learn a poem that can be set to dramatic play and to copy a poem which can be stored in a "fish bowl" pocket to take home.

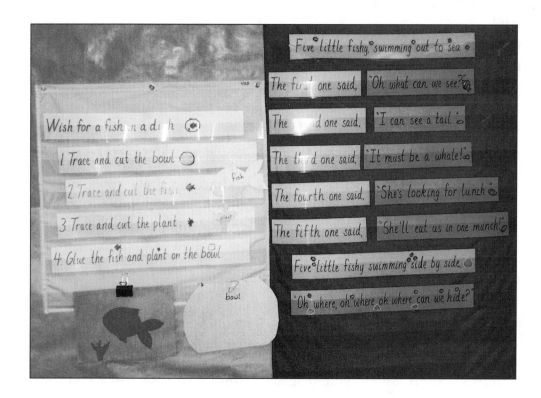

Materials

- 1 24" x 24" and 1 34" x 42" pocket chart
- 5 white and yellow tag quality sentence strips
- 6 blue tag quality sentence strips
- Permanent marker (for teacher)
- Scissors (for teacher and students)
- Fish, plant and bowl patterns (See pages 89 and 90.)

- Tagboard for templates
- Glue
- 9" x 12" sheets of pale blue construction paper (quantity depends on children in class)
- 6" x 6" pieces of orange construction paper
- 4" x 4" pieces of green construction paper
- 9" x 12" sheets of lavender or other color construction paper

Pocket Chart Words

(34" x 42" pocket chart)
Five Little Fishy
by Valerie SchifferDanoff
Five little fishy, swimming out to sea
The first one said, "Oh what can
    we see?"
The second one said, "I can see a tail."
The third one said, "It must be
    a whale!"
The fourth one said, "She's looking
    for lunch."
The fifth one said, "She'll eat us in
    one munch!"
Five little fishy swimming side by side,
"Oh where, oh where, oh where can
    we hide?"

(24" x 24" pocket chart)
Wish for a fish in a dish
1. Trace and cut the bowl.
2. Trace and cut the fish.
3. Trace and cut the plant.
4. Glue the fish and plant on the
    bowl.

You can show children how to glue just
the side and bottom edges of the bowl
onto the second piece of 9" x 12" construction paper so that the bowl can
become a pocket for storing the poem
and additional fish.

 ## Setup

1. Write the directions for making the
    fish and bowl on white sentence
    strips. You can draw little pictures on
    the sentence strips, too. Use the pat-
    terns to make templates of the fish,
    plant and bowl.

2. Write the poem on the yellow and
    blue sentence strips. Use yellow for
    the narrative and blue for the dia-
    logue.

3. Place the sentence strips in the pock-
    et charts respectively.

4. Place construction paper, glue and
    scissors near the pocket charts.

5. Read the poem with children. Give
    children turns acting out the poem.

6. Read the directions to children for
    making the fish bowl.

 ## Variation

Children can draw, color and cut out
additional fish to keep in the bowl, and
then use them to act out the poem on
their own.

Literature Integrations

Where's That Fish? by Barbara Brenner
    and Bernice Chardiet (Scholastic,
    1994)

Ten Sly Piranhas by Victoria Chess
    (Penguin, 1993)

Big Al by Andrew Clements (Picture
    Book Studio, 1988)

Ibis A True Whale Story by John
    Himmelman (Scholastic, 1990)

The Rainbow Fish by Marcus Pfister
    (North-South Books, 1992)

Franklin Wants a Pet by Pauleete
    Bourgeois (Scholastic, 1995)

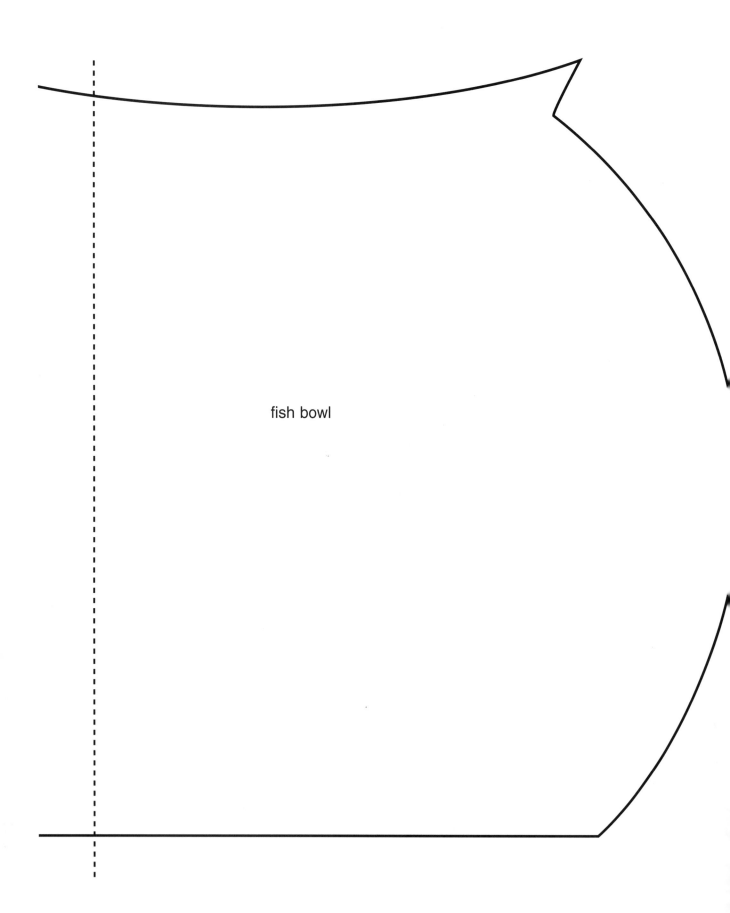

fish bowl

An Elf Is as Small as . . .

Purpose: To experience the concept of size perspective through poetry and the making of an elf.

 **Materials**

- 1 42″ x 58″ pocket chart or 2 34″ x 42″ pocket charts
- 16 tag quality sentence strips in 3 different colors
- Paper sentence strips (amount depends on children in your class)
- Permanent marker (for teacher)
- Elf patterns: hat, legs, shirt, bow and face (See pages 93-95.)
- Tagboard for elf templates
- Scissors and glue (for teacher and children)

1 each of the following for each child:
- 9″ x 12″ sheet of construction paper (in skin tones)
- 9″ x 12″ sheet of construction paper (in assorted colors)
- 12″ x 18″ sheet of construction paper (in assorted colors-optional)

Pocket Chart Words

"The Little Elf" by John Kendrick Bangs
(*St. Nicholas Book of Verse* The Century Co., Appleton Century Crofts, Inc. 1923.

I met a little Elf man once,
Down where the lilies blow.
I asked him why he was so small.
And why he didn't grow.
He slightly frowned, and with his eye
He looked me through and through
"I'm quite as big for me," said he.
"As you are big for you."

An elf is as small as
1. Trace and cut the elf's hat.
2. Trace and cut the elf's face.
3. Trace and cut the elf's shirt.
4. Trace and cut the elf's legs.
5. Glue your elf together.
Draw on eyes, nose, mouth and hair.

Setup

1. Write the poem on sentence strips in alternating colors to highlight rhyming words.

2. Write the elf directions on sentence strips and draw little pictures.

3. Trace the patterns to make templates. Label each template.

4. Make an elf as a model.

5. Place all of the above in the pocket chart(s).

6. Teach the poem and discuss the ideas with children. Children often think they are so very small in an adult world or perhaps just the opposite, bigger than life. This poem and project can give them some perspective.

7. As children complete their elves encourage them to compare the size of their elves to something. Write their responses on paper sentence strips, then glue them with the elf on construction paper to make a class big book or bulletin board display. Sentences might read, "An elf is as small as my baby sister." or "An elf is as tall as my knee."

Literature Integrations

Is a Blue Whale the Biggest Thing There Is? by Robert E. Wells (Albert Whitman & Co., 1993)

Too Much by Dorothy Stott (Penguin, 1990)

The Little Mouse, The Red Ripe Strawberry, and The Big Hungry Bear by Don and Audrey Wood (Child's Play, 1984)

Giant Story by Annegert Fuchahuber (Carolrhoda, 1988)

legs

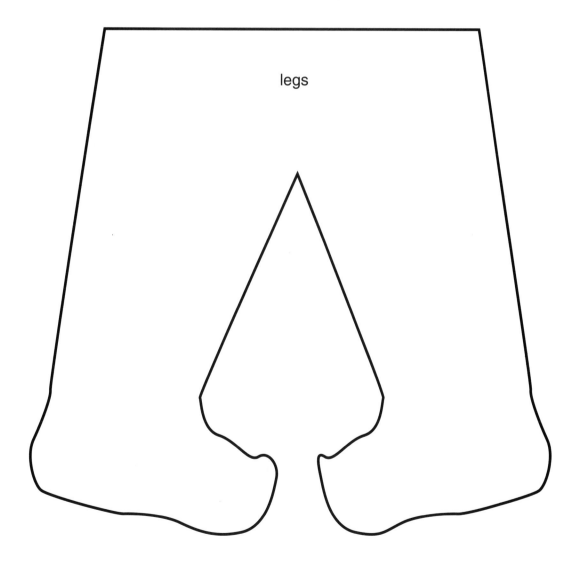

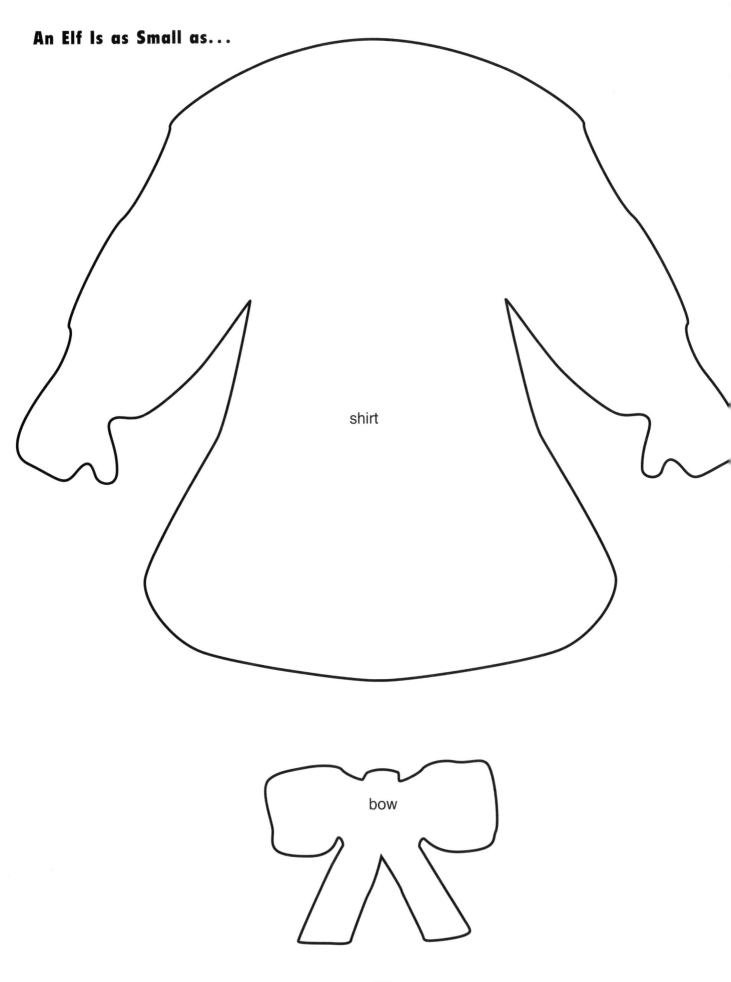

shirt

bow

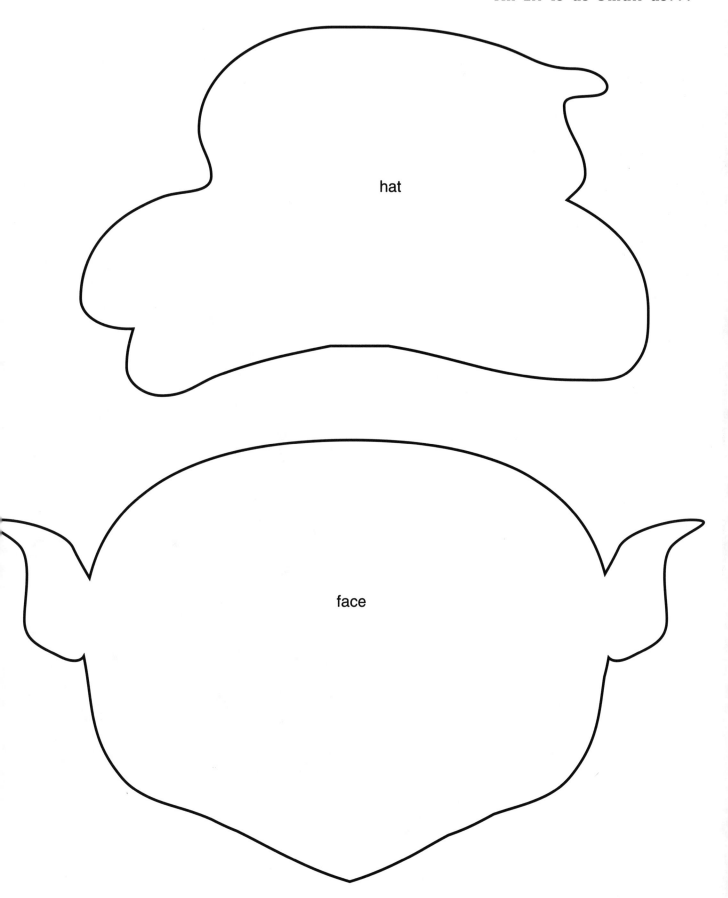

hat

face

A Hamster in My Pocket

Purpose: To appreciate and learn a poem about a well-loved children's pet and make a paper replica of one, complete with a hiding place.

◆ ◆ ◆ Materials ◆ ◆ ◆

- 1 24" x 24" pocket chart and 1 34" x 42" pocket chart (shown) or 1 42" x 58" pocket chart
- 5 blue, 4 yellow and 4 white tag quality sentence strips
- Permanent marker (for teacher)
- Glue
- Scissors (for teacher and children)
- Hamster, pocket and T-shirt patterns (See page 98.)
- Tagboard for templates
- Markers
- Manuscript paper

1 of the following for each child:
- 9" x 12" sheet of construction paper in any color
- 4" x 4" piece of construction paper in any color
- 4" x 4" piece of beige or brown construction paper

96

Pocket Chart Words

(Pocket chart 1)
"Hamsters" by Marci Ridlon (from *Read A-Loud Rhymes for the Very Young* selected by Jack Prelutsky, Alfred A. Knopf, 1986)

Hamsters are the nicest things
That anyone could own.
I like them even better than
Some dogs that I have known.
Their fur is soft, their faces nice.
They're small when they are grown.
And they sit inside your pocket
When you are all alone.

(Pocket chart 2)
A hamster in my pocket
1. Trace and cut two T-shirts.
2. Trace and cut a pocket.
3. Trace and cut a hamster.

Setup

1. Write the words of the poem on sentence strips in alternating colors.

2. Write the directions for the project on sentence strips in another color.

3. Place the sentence strips in the pocket charts.

4. Trace the patterns to make templates for the hamster, the pocket and the T-shirt. Label these and place them in the pocket chart after you make your sample.

5. Read the poem with children. Then share the project. Children can copy the poem onto manuscript paper and store it between the two shirts. Be sure to have children just glue the T-shirts together around the edges and leave the neck unglued for an opening into which they can slide the poem. Children should also only glue the sides and bottom edge of the pocket to allow an opening for the hamster.

Literature Integrations

Franklin Wants A Pet by Paulette Bourgeois (Scholastic, 1995)

Pet Show by Ezra Jack Keats (Macmillan, 1972)

Arthur's Pet Business by Marc Brown (Little Brown & Co. 1990)

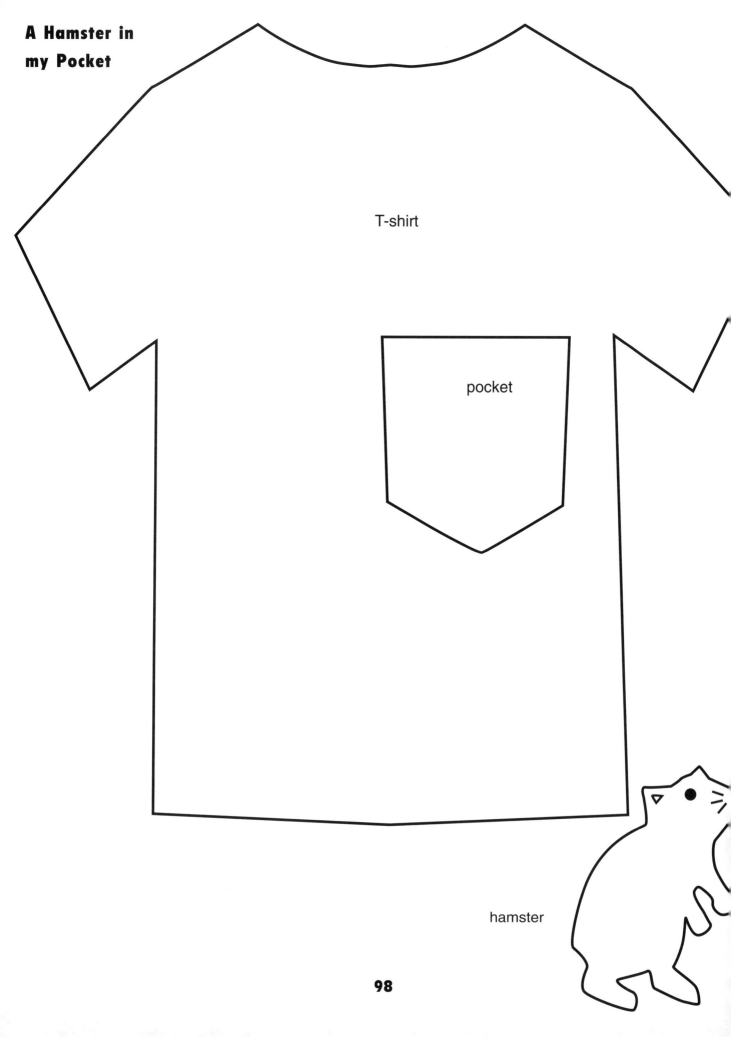

T-shirt

pocket

hamster

CHAPTER SIX

Pocket Charts for an Integrated Unit

As you have seen, pocket charts can be used for many purposes. Pocket charts can be just the spark needed to excite the children in your class to participate in a variety of language arts, math and literature activities. Following are directions for an integrated language arts, math, science and art unit which is based on four poems. The poems are learned and acted out with paper-plate puppets. The poems provide a built in motivation for a two-week math unit. The paper-plate puppets are the hands-on manipulative.

An Integrated Unit

Purpose: To introduce four poems for dramatic play which can then be integrated with math, science and art.

 **Materials**

- 40 tag quality sentence strips in assorted colors (you can decide colors to use for each poem and dialogue)
- Permanent markers in assorted colors
- Monster, goblin, pumpkin, bat and teeth patterns (See pages 110-111.)
- Crayons, scissors, pencils and craft glue (for teacher and children)
- 1 dinner-size paper plate per child
- 2 9" x 10" pieces of lightweight tagboard per child
- 12" x 18" sheets of tagboard in white and assorted colors for the teacher to make monsters, goblins, bats, pumpkins and teeth
- 1 sock per child (ask children to bring these in, the more colorful the better)
- 1 letter-size manila envelope per child
- Assortment pack of high-gloss tagboard (available in art supply stores, but you can substitute lightweight tagboard)
- 4-6 copies of the grid sheet per child (See page 107.)
- 1 copy of the sheet titled "The Four Games" per child (See page 106.)
- 1 copy of each set of teeth cards per child (See pages 108-109.)

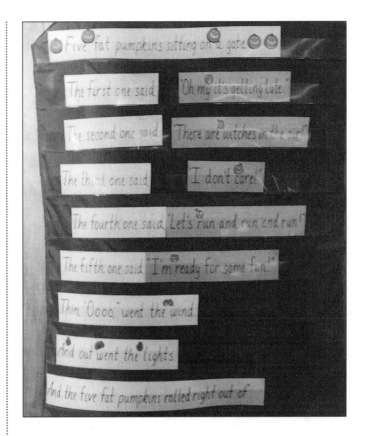

Poems

Pocket Chart Words

If you do not have four pocket charts, you can borrow from other teachers or write the words on sentence strips and mount them on a bulletin board or on mural paper.

(Pocket chart 1)
Five little goblins on a Halloween night
Made a very, very spooky sight.
The first one danced on his tippy-tip-
toes.
The next one tumbled and bumped his
nose.
The next one jumped high up in the air.
The next one walked like a fuzzy bear.
The next one sang a Halloween song.
Five goblins played the whole night
long!
from *Hand Rhymes* collected by Marc Brown, Penguin, 1985.

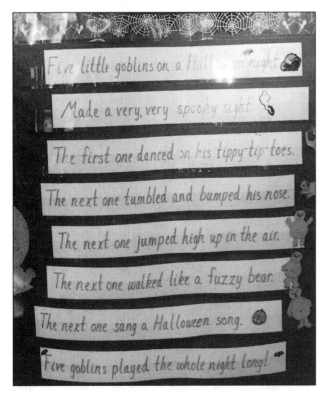

(Pocket chart 2)
Five fat pumpkins sitting on a gate
The first one said, "Oh my it's getting
late."
The second one said, "There are
witches in the air!"
The third one said, "I don't care!"
The fourth one said, "Let's run and
run and run!"
The fifth one said, "I'm ready for some
fun!"
Then, "Oooo" went the wind.
And out went the lights
And the five fat pumpkins rolled right
out of sight.

(Pocket chart 3)

Five batty bats were hanging 'neath the moon.

"Quiet!" said the first. "The witch is coming soon."

"She's green," said the second, "with a purple pointy nose."

"Black boots," said the third, "cover up her ugly toes!"

"Her broom," said the fourth, "can scratch you that I know."

"I'm scared," said the fifth. "I think we'd better go!"

Five batty bats escaped into the night.

"Dear me!" said the witch. "That's a scary sight!"

(Pocket chart 4)

Five little monsters by the light of the moon.

Stirring pudding with a wooden spoon.

The first one says, "It mustn't be runny."

The second one says, "That would make it taste funny."

The third one says, "It mustn't be lumpy."

The fourth one says, "That would make me grumpy."

The fifth one smiles, hums a little tune,

And licks all the drippings from the wooden pudding spoon.

"Five Little Monsters" by Eve Merriam from *Blackberry Ink Poems* by Eve Merriam, William Morrow, 1985.

◆ ◼ ◆ Setup for ◆ ◼ ◆
Dramatic Play
and Art Integration

1. Write all the poems on sentence strips, writing each poem on a different color and using a different color within the poems for the dialogue.

2. Use the patterns to make bats, monsters, goblins and pumpkins to display with the poems.

3. Place poems and cutouts in the pocket charts.

4. Read the four poems with children. There are enough parts for twenty children to each be a character from the poems. If you need more parts, assign children to be narrators or in the case of the bat poem, there's a witch's part. If you need fewer parts, use fewer poems.

5. Have each child choose the poem he or she would like to be in. The children can be flexibly grouped this way, or you can assign each child a part. If you do, having a fluent reader in each group helps.

Hint: If you celebrate Halloween in your classroom, this unit is great for small group guided reading at that time of year. The children are very motivated to practice learning the poems. Grouping and working together cooperatively to practice is a plus!

6. Over a period of 2 to 3 days have each child copy his or her poem. The amount of time needed to copy depends on your grade and class. If you use a reading response journal, that's a perfect place in which to write it. Be sure to point out that this is handwriting practice too! Writing legibly is very important if they're going to read it back to themselves.

◆ ◼ ◆ Setup for ◆ ◼ ◆
Art Integration

1. Using the teeth pattern, make a template and then cut out two sets of teeth from white tagboard for each child in your class.

2. Here comes the fun part! Give each child a paper plate, some high-gloss tagboard, two sets of white teeth, crayons, scissors and glue. Set them **almost** free to create their own monster, goblin, pumpkin or bat.

3. Some definition is needed here. You will need to go around while children are working and glue the socks to their plates. Use plenty of craft glue to attach the sock from the heel to the toe down the center of plate. When the plate is folded the child's hand goes into the sock so that he or she can work the plate like a mouth opening and closing.

4. Children making pumpkins and bats might need to be reminded that pumpkins are orange, and bats are brown or black. Having real photos on hand helps. To make cutouts of eyes and ears stand up, they need a fold as a tab to glue to the plate. You'll see the teeth pattern shows how this is done. The teeth are glued along the inner edges of what will become the character's mouth. Most children colored that inside part a reddish tone.

5. Once the glue is fairly dry, children can color both sides of their plates.

6. When the puppets are complete, children can rehearse the poems with them. Then invite another class to view the performance. Children loved these simple plate puppets and were encouraged to keep them at their seats during the entire two-week period it took for this unit to be completed.

◆ ■ ◆ Setup for ◆ ■ ◆ Math Integration

1. Using the teeth on the paper-plate puppets have the class count by fives together. Child one will count 5, 10. Child two will continue with 15, 20. Continue until you count all the puppet teeth in the classroom. A hundreds chart is very good to have on hand for this activity. Or you can write numbers down as they count. Teach children to count on, using the teeth as a manipulative. Child three might say "21, 22, 23, 24, **25**!" then "26, 27, 28, 29, **30**!" The number you get up to will depend on the number of children in your class.

2. Copy the two sets of teeth cards for each child and yourself. If lightweight tagboard is not available to you or your copy machine will not copy that, use paper and caution the children to take great care.

3. Give each child the two sets of teeth cards and have them carefully cut them apart on the lines. Explain that these are playing cards. Have children store the playing cards in the manila envelope.

4. Teach the four games using the directions on "The Four Games" sheet. Be sure to model each game with the whole class. Give each child one grid sheet at a time as you teach and model each game. Pick the cards or go around the class and have children pick the cards while the whole class writes the same number together on their individual grid sheets.

5. Children can be given additional grid sheets to play the games in groups of two or more. Then send a copy of "The Four Games" sheet, the two sets of teeth cards and a grid sheet home in the envelope along with the puppet. Parents can make additional copies of the grid sheet if they like.

◆ ■ ■ Science ◆ ■ ■ and Literature Integration

Integrate science by reading fiction and nonfiction books such as those listed below. Your focus can be on teeth and animal classifications by teeth.

Giant Dinosaurs by Erna Rowe (Scholastic, 1973)

What Big Teeth You Have! by Patricia Lauber (HarperCollins, 1986)

Loose Tooth by Steven Kroll (Holiday House, 1984)

Doctor DeSoto by William Steig (Farrar, Straus & Giroux, 1982)

Doctor DeSoto Goes to Africa by William Steig (HarperCollins, 1992)

■ ■ ■ Poetry Integration

Since children in kindergarten, first and second grade are sure to be losing teeth, you might want to try the following poem.

A tooth fell out and left a space,
So big my tongue can touch my face.
And every time I smile, I show
A space where something used to grow.
I miss my tooth as you can guess.
But then I have to brush one less.

from *Creative Activities for Young Children* (Delmar, 1985)

The Four Games

Count On

- Number the first row of eight squares from 1-8.
- Pick cards and count on until you reach the last square which will be numbered 80.

Add Up to 10

- Turn the paper so a row with 10 squares is at the top.
- 1 or 2 players choose cards numbering the squares row by row.
- The first player to reach 10 wins the row. If playing by yourself, play until you number the whole row.
- Which numbers did you add together to reach 10?

Count Down

- Turn the paper so a row with 10 squares is at the top.
- Number the last 10 squares counting down from 80 to 71.
- Then choose cards and count down by the number chosen until you get to 1.

Count Down from 10

(1 or 2 players)
- Turn the paper so a row with 10 squares is at the top.
- Write the number 10 at the end of each row.
- Choose cards and count down from ten.
- If two players play, the first player to reach the end of the row wins the row.

1 One	**6** Six
2 Two	**7** Seven
3 Three	**8** Eight
4 Four	**9** Nine
5 Five	**10** Ten

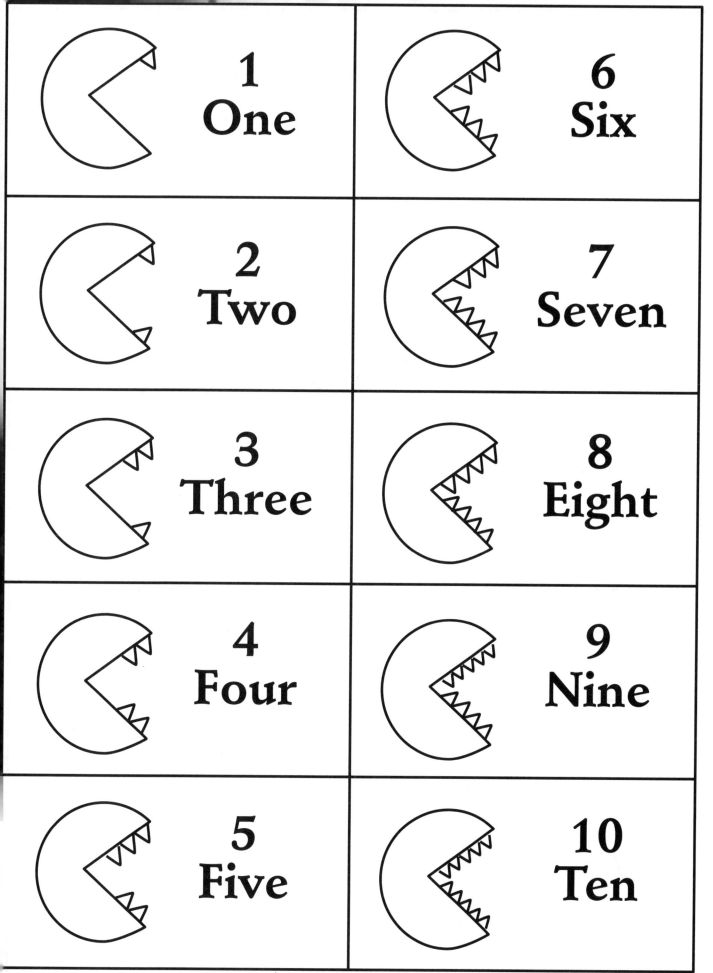

1 One	**6** Six
2 Two	**7** Seven
3 Three	**8** Eight
4 Four	**9** Nine
5 Five	**10** Ten

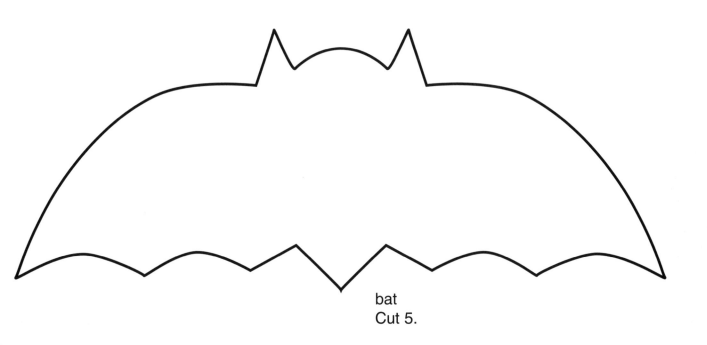

bat
Cut 5.